Wandering Educators Press

Vietnam: 100 Unusual Travel Tips and a Guide to Living and Working There

By Barbara Adam and Vu Vo

Table of Contents

Preface

Vietnam: a country of extraordinary food and friendly people; of turbulent history and natural beauty. With this book, you hold an insider's guide to discovering the best of Vietnam – and, when you fall in love with the country, a guide to moving there. It's a glimpse into a deep and complex culture that has a long, rich history. Written by an Australian expat who moved to Vietnam – and is now ensconced there, complete with husband and family (the remarkable photos and cultural fact-checking are by her Vietnamese husband), it's truly a cross-cultural guide like no other. We're proud to publish this with Wandering Educators Press – and share Vietnam with our readers.

Dr. Jessie Voigts, Publisher, WanderingEducators.com

This is a book that attempts the nearly impossible -- explaining Vietnam to an outsider. The country is a fascinating mix of old and new, urban and rural, Communism and capitalism, with wafts of Chinese and French influence. It's a country full of internet-savvy mobile phone-toting young people -- 60% of the population is under 40 -- who still follow the ancient practices of honoring their parents and their dead ancestors.

It's not a book full of lists of things to see and do. (Although there are a few recommendations about what to eat.) This book is intended to explain everyday life in Vietnam, a life you will see glimpses of during your visit to this crazy, chaotic, intriguing and often overwhelming Southeast Asian nation. It's also a guide to the practicalities of visiting and living in Vietnam

Use this book as a companion to a travel guidebook to understand Vietnam, so you can navigate some of the craziness a little better and make some sense of some of the things you'll see. I just love the place and I hope you do too.

Barbara Adam, author

During my lifetime, Vietnam has changed so much and sometimes it seems there's something new to discover every day. I love my country so much that in my 20s I took time off work -- much to the horror of my friends and family -- to travel from the south to the north and back again. I embarked on a new journey of discovery when I met Barbara and began showing her "my" Vietnam. Through her eyes, I experienced many things afresh and also came to realize how unique my country is. Together, we discovered a love of introducing "our" Vietnam to visitors through our street food tours - and now through this book. I hope we are able to help you come to love Vietnam as much as we do.

Vu Vo, fact-checker and photographer

Introduction

In 2007, during a cycling trip with my dad for his 60th, I was bewitched by the energy and exotic charm of Vietnam; its bustling chaotic cities, incense-scented temples and emerald green rice fields.

Four months after that cycle trip, I flew back to Vietnam on a one-way ticket, hoping to recapture that elusive holiday feeling and hold onto it for good.

I'd chucked in my job as a political reporter in Australia, sold my car, put my stuff into storage and enrolled in a four-week Teaching English as a Second Language (TESOL) course in Ho Chi Minh City. I was starting a new, more carefree life.

After making such a radical life change, I wasn't really expecting to embark on a whole series of life changes. But that's what happened. I taught English for a little while (and didn't really enjoy it), worked for an English-language newspaper, made friends, learned about Vietnam, studied Vietnamese and met a cute guy. There didn't seem to be any reason to leave.

Things got serious with the cute guy and I was offered a new job. The years flew by, with trips around Asia and visits home to introduce Darling Man to the parents and friends. We decided to add a baby to the mix - the icing on the cake.

The baby came along and the job disappeared, so we moved to Singapore to try the career thing again as an expat family. After a while, we decided to shake things up *again* and try location independence, basing ourselves in Chiang Mai in northern Thailand and planning a working holiday in Europe.

But Vietnam called us back, and here we are in Ho Chi Minh City again, running street food tours through our company Saigon Street Eats, and chasing TWO little ones around. I exercise my writing muscles with travel and food writing, a little corporate corporate work and a blog about my crazy post-career life, The Dropout Diaries.

Here are **100 Tips for Travel in Vietnam** – allowing you to make the most of your stay – and a **guide for moving there**, in case you fall in love with the country, too.

Ho Chi Minh City flower market

Basket boats at Quy Nhon

ABOUT VIETNAM

Geography, culture and history

Vietnam is a long thin S-shaped country that takes in the tail end of the majestic Himalaya near its northern border with China and sweeps downwards along the coast to the fertile plains of the Mekong Delta, the country's rice bowl.

Squashed between the sea in the east and Laos and Cambodia to the west, Vietnam is a land of contrasts, with bustling noisy cities and timeless pastoral scenes. It's a one-party state ruled by the Communist Party of Vietnam. Corruption is rampant and the bureaucracy is slow and inefficient but the economy is growing and everyone, it seems, is on the make, with sights set on untold riches, fame and fortune - if only they can study hard enough, work long enough or come up with the next brilliant idea.

Vietnam is a country that opted out of global progress for a while, then opted back in. And so the old guy you see in dusty tattered clothes doesn't think it's odd that he's talking on a mobile phone as he trudges along behind his buffalo on the edge of a rutted track. These old world-new world clashes are what I love about Vietnam and the Vietnamese people.

Vietnam is a land where glass and chrome skyscrapers tower over the cities while farmers still plant rice by hand. In the traffic, grandmothers ride motorbikes in their pajamas beside stunningly beautiful girls with false eyelashes and flawless makeup. It's a place where seemingly gentle people delight in eating dog, cat, snake, field mouse and turtle. Yet many Buddhists go meat-free twice a month. It's a nation of skinny people who always seem to be eating (and if they're not actually eating, they're talking about their next meal). And everywhere, just everywhere, the entrepreneurial spirit is alive and well – from children selling chewing gum and flowers on the streets to people pushing homemade magnetic trolleys through the traffic to collect slivers of metal to sell for scrap.

There are an estimated 93 million people living in Vietnam, the 14th most populous country in the world. Seventy percent of the population lives outside the urban areas, and agriculture is still a key part of the economy.

China ruled Vietnam for 1,000 years and there are many cultural and social elements of Vietnamese society that can be traced back to China, such as ancestor worship, the Chinese zodiac and certain celebrations, such as *Tết,* the lunar new year.

Tet decorations

The Kinh are the ethnic majority in Vietnam, representing more than 80% of the population. As well as the Kinh, there are 53 other recognized ethnic groups, with their own languages, customs and traditional dress.

Vietnam has 63 provinces, including five cities with provincial status, which are further divided into wards, communes and villages. Addresses can get pretty long in Vietnam.

The country is informally divided up into general geographic regions – the north, the south and central Vietnam. There's also the Central Highlands (the elevated inland part of central Vietnam) and the Mekong Delta in the south.

Flower H'mong girls at the Bac Ha Market in Vietnam's far north

Hanoi, in the north, is the capital and is regarded as the country's political and cultural hub. Ho Chi Minh City, in the south, is considered the financial and business center.

After the end of the American War (known as the Vietnam War outside of Vietnam) in 1975, the city formerly known as Saigon was renamed after Ho Chi Minh, who founded the Communist Party of Vietnam and led the uprising against the colonial French rulers. Uncle Ho, as he's fondly known, died in 1969 at the age of 79, without seeing his dream of a united independent Vietnam become a reality.

Colonial-style decor

The tourist trail

Because Vietnam is such a long skinny country, most tourists follow a well-worn route between Hanoi and Ho Chi Minh City.

Basket boats on the beach at Con Dao Island

The north and south of Vietnam are connected by **Highway 1,** which runs all the way from Hanoi to Ho Chi Minh City, as well as the **Reunification Express**, the main train line, which takes about 33 hours to travel between Vietnam's two major cities.

TIP: I personally recommend a south-north route, starting in Ho Chi Minh City and taking some time to dip down into the verdant Mekong Delta and/or taking a relaxing break on Phu Quoc or Con Dao islands before heading north towards Hanoi.

Starting in the southern city of Ho Chi Minh City means your first impression of Vietnam will be one of utter urban chaos -- and lots of smiles. You'll get used to the sensory overload of metropolitan Vietnam before having to deal with the stony-faced grumpiness that seems to prevail in Hanoi. Vietnam's capital is also notorious among travelers for the pushy money-hungry street vendors who congregate in the city's tourist area. Grumpy people and pushy vendors exist all over Vietnam -- and all over the world -- but from my experience and from all the anecdotes I've heard, Hanoi is distinctly less friendly to tourists than Ho Chi Minh City.

(My south-north advice has been challenged by some of my friends, who say starting in the north means that your experiences get better as you move south. I guess the essence of my advice is not to have high expectations of Hanoi, which does have a unique charm despite my gloomy warnings.)

Con Dao sunset

If you start your tour in Ho Chi Minh City, the main stopping points on the way to Hanoi are:

- the seaside resort town of Nha Trang;

- the former French hill station of Dalat;

- the revitalized commercial city of Danang, only 20 minutes from the World Heritage-listed former port town of Hoi An;

- Hoi An with its "ancient town" center that's barely changed since the 17th century; and

- the former Imperial capital of Hue.

(There are, of course, many other smaller towns that are well worth exploring; these places are just the most popular destinations.)

Here's a little bit more detail about the major stops on the south-north tourist trail:

The coastal city of **Nha Trang,** a popular vacation spot for Russian tourists, is known for its nightlife, as well as for being Vietnam's scuba diving capital. Other highlights include the Po Nagar Cham Towers and the new super-fancy Vinpearl Amusement Park, linked to the mainland by cable car.

> TIP: Vinpearl Amusement Park is a great day out for families, and you do need to allocate a full day. There are a range of rides, an arcade area (included in the entry price), an oceanarium and a water park with slides and various pools. The cable car ride there is the world's longest and gives you stunning views of Nha Trang and the coastline.

Danang, the largest city in central Vietnam, is one of the country's most important ports and the site of an international airport. One of Danang's beaches, Non Nuoc Beach, was called China Beach by American Troops during the Vietnam War (known as the American War in Vietnam) and was a popular spot for GIs to get a bit of R&R. It's still a popular spot, with many five-star resorts lining the beach.

Hoi An, 30 minutes by taxi from the Danang International Airport, is a World Heritage-listed port city with a colorful history. Tourism is the main industry here and the city has also made a name for itself as a center for tailoring. Hoi An, with its laid back atmosphere, historic architecture, gracious river esplanade and two white sand beaches, is an idyllic place for an extended stay. Golf nuts can get their fix at one of the world class golf courses in the area, divers can get theirs off Cham Island, and food lovers, well, they will think they've died and gone to heaven. There are also many interesting day trips to nearby islands, mangrove areas, and the Cham ruins of My Son. On the downside, Hoi An is prone to flooding and there is a very dangerous whirlpool at Cua Dai Beach – keep an eye out for the warning sign in English.

> TIP: Hoi An has a number of must-try local dishes, including the "white rose" prawn rice-flour dumpling and the seriously addictive *cao lầu* pork noodle soup. One of my all-time favourite Vietnamese dishes is *mì Quảng,* which is a tasty half-salad half-soup noodle dish. The best *mì Quảng* in town (in my opinion) is at Quan Hai, 6A Truong Minh Street.

Hue, on the banks of the Perfume River, is the former imperial capital of Vietnam and home to the exotically named Forbidden Purple Palace within the Citadel. Unfortunately, the Forbidden Purple Palace was extensively damaged during the American War, and then neglected. Restoration work is ongoing, although what remains is only a charcoal sketch of the original. A video in the visitor center shows what the place would have looked like when Vietnam's royal dynasties ruled.

Hue is also home to the tombs of the emperors, built by the emperors themselves while they were alive.

TIP: Attempting to visit all the tombs can bring on a bad case of tomb fatigue. I like the tomb of Tu Duc, who ruled from 1848 to 1883. Tu Duc had the longest rein of any monarch in the Nguyen Dynasty. He had 100 wives and concubines, yet no biological children (an adopted son assumed the throne after his death). Tu Duc used his tomb as a second home, reciting poetry in the lakeside pavilion and hunting for game on the small island at the centre of the lake. (Ironically, Tu Duc's adopted son is buried at the site but the whereabouts of Tu Duc's grave remains a secret. He was buried elsewhere to deter grave robbers.) The sprawling grounds and various buildings of this tomb are great for exploring and imagining the romantic and extravagant life of Vietnam's former ruling elite.

TIP: Hue specializes in bite-size cuisine. You get many bites per plate but don't be afraid to order another serve. The must-try dishes of the former Imperial capital are:

- *Ram ít* - a tiny prawn encased in crunchy batter, topped with a soft rice pancake and a sprinkle of ground prawn

- *Bánh bèo* - a little rice flour pancake topped with chopped prawn, ground dried prawn and a square of fried pork fat, a garnish I call the Vietnamese crouton

- *Bánh khoái* - a fried pancake stuffed with prawns and crunchy bean sprouts, served with a range of side dishes, including slices of tart Hue guava, lettuce, herbs and a

tangy dipping sauce

- *Chả tôm* - a prawn version of the fish cake

The main rail and road routes linking Ho Chi Minh City and Hanoi bypass Vietnam's picturesque Central Highlands, the centerpiece of which is **Dalat**, an elevated getaway that's a welcome escape from the tropical steamy weather at sea level.

Swan-shaped pedal boats in Dalat

Once known as *Le Petit Paris*, Dalat is surrounded by rolling pine-covered hills. It has many French colonial buildings, a magnificent lake, gardens, a mini replica of the Eiffel Tower and the summer palace of the last emperor of Vietnam, Bao Dai. There's even a golf course, originally opened in 1922 with the support of Emperor Bao Dai.

TIP: The domestic airport servicing Dalat, Lien Khuong, is about 28 kms from the city. There are regular flights between Dalat and Ho Chi Minh City, Hanoi, Danang and Vinh. The bus from Ho Chi Minh City to Dalat takes seven to nine hours, depending on the traffic. Sleeper buses are also available. Note that the twisting mountain roads can be a bit startling on a bus.

Dalat is famous for its flowers, including beautifully fragrant roses

Often overlooked by tourists, the seaside city of **Vung Tau** is one of my favorite getaways from Ho Chi Minh City. The beach is only OK, nothing like the clichéd Southeast Asian tropical beaches. The appeal of Vung Tau is its quirkiness. It has a giant Jesus statue, enormous dragon-shaped hedges, tandem "love" bicycles for hire, semi-pornographic statues in its ocean-front park, dozens of peaceful Buddhist temples and some of the best seafood in Vietnam.

TIP: Vung Tau is only a 75-minute ferry trip from Ho Chi Minh City but the ferry schedule takes no heed of when tourists and commuters would like to arrive and depart -- the last ferries each way depart at 4.30pm, making for a very short day trip. Plan to stay at least one night in Vung Tau to soak up some of the town's eccentricities.

TIP: Vung Tau's local food specialty is *bánh khọt*, a small fried pancake made from rice flour and topped with a prawn and green onion. The pancakes are wrapped in mustard leaves with shredded papaya and a range of aromatic Vietnamese herbs and dipped in a sweet fish sauce-based dipping sauce.

TIP: The seaside city of Vung Tau is also famous for its longans, a fruit that tastes like a sherry-flavored lychee. They're available in Vung Tau year round, although June and July are considered the best longan months. Longans are also known as dragon's eyeballs and once you remove the brown peel to uncover the glistening inner part of the fruit you'll see why.

Longans for sale beachside in Vung Tau

Mui Ne is another seaside resort town accessible from Ho Chi Minh City. It lies between Nha Trang and Ho Chi Minh City and is a popular stopping-off point for travelers on the tourist trail. It's only 230 kms (143 miles) from Ho Chi Minh City but it takes five to seven hours to get there because of the state of the roads and the corresponding low speed limit on the highway.

The beachfront strip at Mui Ne is designed for tourists as a place to wind down, relax and walk along the beach. (If it's there. Often the sea has shifted the sand, leaving the not-so-pretty concrete breakwater exposed). Before the tourist hordes arrived, there wasn't much to Mui Ne, which was just an outlying suburb of the fishing village of Phan Thiet. Mui Ne is home to colored sand dunes, where local children congregate to rent plastic mats to slide down the dunes on.

TIP: There's a reason Mui Ne has made a name for itself in the kite-surfing world -- it can be very windy! When the wind is up, being outdoors on or near the beach is not much fun. Windy season (also known as winter or the dry season) is November to April. During the windy season, the breeze is usually mild in the morning and gains strength until lunch time, stays strong for about three hours and then begins to taper off again. You can find information about the wind speed and direction on windguru.cz.

TIP: Mui Ne is in Binh Thuan Province, where dragon fruit farms abound. There are two types of dragon fruit, both a similar startlingly pink on the outside. The more common dragon fruit is white on the inside, the rarer variety is a deep pink-red. Dragon fruit grow on a snake-like cactus, usually planted on top of a pole for easier access. Dragon fruit season used to be March to August but farmers can now produce the fruit year-round. Some farmers around Mui Ne use lights at night in the "off" season to encourage fruiting when selling prices are higher.

The impossibly green rice paddies and conical-hatted women of the **Mekong Delta** are some of the most iconic images of Vietnam. The mighty Mekong River flows from the Tibetan Plateau through China, Myanmar, Laos, Thailand, Cambodia and Vietnam to feed the delta, known as Vietnam's rice bowl. The Mekong Delta area produces half of the nation's rice crop, which is *a lot* of rice, considering Vietnam is the world's second-largest rice exporter after Thailand.

> TIP: Beware of booking super-cheap Mekong tours through travel agents in Ho Chi Minh City's backpacker district. Most of the unbelievably priced tours involve visits to brick, rice paper and coconut candy factories, dire musical performances and very average food. When it comes to Mekong Delta tours, you get what you pay for. It's worth paying more to get a worthwhile experience.

From Hanoi, many visitors take side trips to **Sapa** - the picturesque former hill station near the country's highest peak, Mount Fansipan - and the World Heritage-listed **Halong Bay**, which is studded with amazing limestone karsts.

> TIP: Halong Bay is beautiful but it has a shocking safety record and tour operators (those offering the cheaper tours) have a tendency to treat tourists like bothersome sheep that just need to be shipped from here to there. I personally prefer Sapa over Halong Bay, for its mountain views and the enterprising local ethnic minority people who find ways to profit from their traditional way of life.

A Black H'mong lady at the Sapa Market

History

Vietnam has a long and quite violent history. This small country kept its enormous and powerful northern neighbor, China, at bay for centuries but has, at various times, fallen under Chinese and French rule, as well as Japanese occupation. In the distant past, most of Central Vietnam belonged to the mysterious Hindu Kingdom of Champa, while the Khmer empire that built the temples of Angkor Wat in Cambodia ruled what is now Southern Vietnam.

Vietnam was ruled by the Chinese four times during its 2,700 year history, adding up to a total of 10 centuries of Chinese rule. In 1858, the French invaded and by the turn of the century, the French governed Vietnam, Cambodia, and Laos, calling the region Indochina (*Indochine* in French).

During World War II, the French still ruled Indochina, although the Japanese occupied Vietnam from 1940 to 1945.

In 1941, Ho Chi Minh began a revolt against the French and the Japanese, which led to the Democratic Republic of Vietnam being established in September 1945.

In 1954, under the Geneva Accords, Vietnam was divided into north and south at the 17th parallel. The north was communist and the south non-communist. The U.S., which regarded communism as a great threat to global stability, began providing "advisors" and then military support for the government of South Vietnam. The U.S. never officially declared war on northern Vietnam, but more and more troops were sent over and military action escalated. In 1973, U.S. troops were withdrawn after a cease-fire agreement and two years later, the north declared victory and began reprisals.

The Vietnam-American War ended when North Vietnamese tanks crashed through the gates of the Independence Palace in Ho Chi Minh City. The tanks remain on display at the palace, one of the city's must-see tourist sites.

After the north took control of the south, thousands of Vietnamese people fled their homeland, mostly southern Vietnamese escaping the deprivations and punishments of the northern government. They were the boat people, the desperate and hardworking families who created the Vietnamese diaspora. An estimated two million Vietnamese people left Vietnam on rickety old boats. They and their descendants are now known as *Việt Kiều*, or Overseas Vietnamese, who now have somewhat of a celebrity status in Vietnam. Although some Vietnamese people resent the fact that they fled and so escaped the worst times of the harsh Communist rule, it's acknowledged that the *Việt Kiều*, the now-rich cousins, have done well in the West through assimilation, education, hard work and simply earning a Western salary.

From 1975 to 1986, life was tough in Vietnam. Just about every aspect of life was regulated and religion was discouraged. A coupon system was in force, making it necessary to get some form of official approval for everything from selling home-grown vegetables to getting a bicycle repaired.

In 1986, the Vietnamese government initiated its *đổi mới* or "renovation" policy, moving towards a more liberal and open economy.

Vietnam remains a one-party state, holding parliamentary elections every five years in which the Communist Party of Vietnam is the only party allowed to stand candidates. It is following China's lead in moving towards a market economy but is also wary of China, its big bullying neighbor of the north.

The U.S. lifted its trade embargo on Vietnam in 1994, and a year later U.S. President Bill Clinton announced "normalized" diplomatic relations with Vietnam. These events marked the start of inbound tourism for Vietnam.

Vietnam joined the World Trade Organization in 2007.

WHEN TO VISIT

Vietnam welcomes visitors year-round. There are several tourist "seasons" which depend on the weather, the school holidays and/or summer vacations around the world.

> TIP: Check if you'll be traveling during *Tết* (the dates changes from year to year, depending on the lunar calendar). Outside of the main tourist areas, just about all businesses will be shut for five to seven days over *Tết*. In the main tourist centers, you won't starve but the food options will be limited.

Weather

Vietnam has sweltering tropical weather in the south, cooler climes in the mountains, and in the north, a distinct winter from November to April.

There are two monsoons that affect the weather in Vietnam - the winter monsoon in the country's northeast and the summer monsoon that affects most of the country.

Ho Chi Minh City, in the south (and therefore closer to the equator), has two seasons – hot, and hot and wet. The hot and wet season, also known as the rainy season, runs from May to November. The coolest months are December and January, when night-time temperatures can fall as low as 21 degrees Celsius (70F) and reach about 32 Celsius (89F) during the day. For the rest of the year, the temperature is a pretty steady (and steamy) 24 to 34 degrees Celsius (75-93F).

> TIP: Consider visiting Ho Chi Minh City in the rainy season. The rain is warm, so getting wet is not such a big deal. It rains almost every day but it doesn't rain all day. Most mornings you can set out under clear skies carrying a cheap rain poncho for when the heavens open. Whiling away a rain

storm in a coffee shop can be quite fun. Just be aware that parts of Ho Chi Minh City flood when heavy rains coincide with a king tide (the Saigon River is tidal). Stay out of the flood waters if you have any open wounds on your feet or legs and, even if you don't, wash your skin with soap once you get back to your hotel. You never know what nastiness is going to wash up out of the drains when it floods.

The beaches of Central Vietnam are beautiful but make sure you check the weather forecast.

Central Vietnam is often battered by typhoons during the rainy season from September to January. Strong winds, flooding and mudslides are common, and roads and the rail line are regularly submerged or washed away.

TIP: Keep an eye on weather forecasts if traveling in central Vietnam during the typhoon season. You can check www.tropicalstormrisk.com to see if there are any large storms in the vicinity. Be aware that if a tropical storm or typhoon is headed your way, trains, buses and flights out of the area are likely to be booked up extremely quickly. You could get lucky and snag a ride out of town but if you're traveling in storm season, you may have to ride out the bad weather along with the locals.

Even within the area considered Central Vietnam, the weather varies quite a bit. Around Hue, which is known for its wet weather, the rainy season is from May to December, with the typhoon season around September/October.

In Danang/Hoi An, the wet season runs from September to January, with typhoon season usually in October and November. Hoi An often floods during the typhoon season and some expats organize their trips home during flooding season. The hottest months are usually June to August.

Dalat in the Central Highlands, 1,500 meters above sea level, is cool year-round, with a rainy season that runs from May to November. During this time, roads are often washed out. The coolest season is between November and January, with temperatures of between 14 and 27 degrees Celsius (57-80F).

In Hanoi, the cool and foggy winter is from November to March and the hot and rainy summers run from April to October.

Average temperatures:

Hanoi
January – 14-19 degrees Celsius (58-66 F)

June/July – 27-32 degrees Celsius (80-90 F)

Ho Chi Minh City
January – 22-31 degrees Celsius (72-88 F)

June/July – 25-32 degrees Celsius (77-89 F)

Riding in the rain without a poncho

Public holidays

	2016	2017
New Year's Day	Jan 1	Jan 2
Têt (Lunar New Year)	Feb 8-13	Jan 27-Feb 1
Hung King Festival	Apr 16	Apr 6
Liberation Day	May 2	May 1
Labor Day	May 1	May 1
National Day	Sept 2	Sept 4

WHAT YOU NEED TO ENTER

The government has been tinkering with the visa rules recently to try to boost tourism numbers. Visa rules and fees can change overnight, so do take an effort to ensure you have current information.

To enter Vietnam you need at least one months validity on your passport and at least two blank pages.

Since late 2105, people with passports issued by France, Germany, the UK, Italy, Spain, Denmark, Finland, Norway, Russia, Belarus, Sweden, Japan and South Korea can stay in Vietnam for up to 15 days without a visa. This new visa exemption regulation will remain in place until at least mid-2016 and may or may not be extended. If you qualify for this exemption, you'll need to pay a $5 stamping fee on arrival, but there is no need to provide any supporting documentation or passport photos.

Note: Those who are granted the 15-day visa exemption must be out of the country for at least 30 days before being granted a subsequent visa exemption.

Citizens of Thailand, Singapore, Malaysia, Indonesia, Cambodia and Laos are allowed to stay for up to 30 days without a visa.

Viet Kieu (Overseas Vietnamese), their foreign spouses and children are also now able to visit Vietnam without a visa.

If you still need a visa because your nationality isn't on the visa exemption list or you want to stay longer than the visa exemption you're eligible for, you can get a visa the old-fashioned way: from a Vietnamese embassy or consulate in your home country; or you can organize a visa-on-arrival, which is only available to people arriving by air. There are various agencies offering visa on arrival services

> TIP: The visa on arrival is not well named at all. It is more a letter of invitation that you need to print out and present to the airport customs office. Even with the letter of invitation, you're required to wait while someone physically prepares your visa and sticks it in your passport. Then you pay for the visa. The process can take as little as 15 minutes or as long as two hours, depending on how many international flights arrive at the same time. The visa on arrival processing area is, as you would expect, signposted as "landing visa".

> If you opt for a visa-on-arrival (which often works out cheaper than an old-fashioned visa), make sure you read the instructions carefully and print out the paperwork as per the visa company's instructions. You pay the online visa company for arranging the visa, then you pay the customs office at the airport for the actual visa.

In early 2014, the government announced an "official" online service that lets you fill out an online application form and collect the visa from your nearest Vietnamese embassy or consulate.

There are two types of entry visas – tourist and business. (More information about the business visa and visa extensions is in the Moving to Vietnam section of the book.)

Tourist visas are usually single-entry one month or three-month visas. It's possible to extend these visas if you'd like to stay longer than a month, and it's also possible to organize a re-entry visa if you want to take a quick trip over a border. Local travel agents can organize visa extensions and re-entry visas in about three days for a small fee.

33

It's also possible to get multiple entry tourist visas, which are more expensive than the single entry.

> TIP: Friends have used www.myvietnamvisa.com and www.vietnamvisapro.com for online visas on arrival (Vietnam Visa Pro offers the multiple entry option). These visa companies charge a service fee for arranging the visa. You still have to pay for the actual visa once you arrive in Vietnam.

> TIP: Check the expiry date on your visa the moment the customs officers hands it back to you. Some customs officials calculate the 30 or 90 days exactly, others just give you a month or three months. This can be a problem if you're arriving in February because you'll have less than 30 days, which could mean you'll be overstaying your visa if you've booked to leave the country exactly 30 days after arriving.

HOW TO GET THERE

Vietnam has nine international airports, although the majority don't receive any scheduled international flights, only chartered flights from time to time. The main ports of entry into Vietnam are Noi Bai International Airport (HAN) in the capital Hanoi, and Tan Son Nhat International Airport (SGN) in the nation's commercial hub of Ho Chi Minh City.

The other international airports are:

- Can Tho International Airport (VCA) in Can Tho in the Mekong Delta
- Lien Khuong International Airport (DLI) in Dalat in the Central Highlands
- Danang International Airport (DAD) in Danang in Central Vietnam
- Cat Bi International Airport (HPH) in the northern city of Hai Phong, the main gateway to Halong Bay

- Phu Bai International Airport (HUI) in Hue in Central Vietnam
- Cam Ranh International Airport (CXR) in Nha Trang in Central Vietnam
- Phu Quoc International Airport (PQC) on the southern resort island of Phu Quoc

TIP: Nha Trang, Vietnam's third-biggest international airport, welcomes flights from China, South Korea, Hong Kong, Taiwan, Laos and Cambodia.

TIP: The airports in Can Tho, Dalat, Hai Phong, Hue and Phu Quoc are considered "international" but information about when or if international flights will ever use the airport is sketchy. It's worth double-checking to see if international flights to these destinations have begun. They could be a cheaper entry point into Vietnam than the main hubs.

Vietnam also has a number of land borders shared with China, Laos and Cambodia.

Vietnam's border crossings are:

To/from Cambodia:

- Moc Bai border - crossed when traveling by bus from Ho Chi Minh City to Phnom Penh, the capital of Cambodia.

- Vinh Xuong border - crossed when traveling by boat from the Mekong Delta town of Chau Doc to Phnom Penh.

- Tinh Bien border - this rarely used crossing links Ha Tien in the Mekong Delta with Kampot or Takeo in Cambodia.

To/from China:

- Lao Cai-Ha Hekou border - crossed when traveling between Sapa in northern Vietnam and the Chinese city of Kunming, also crossed when taking the train from Hanoi to Kunming.

- Mong Cai-Dongxing border - this out-of-the-way crossing links the Vietnamese border town of Mong Cai in Quang Ninh province with the Chinese border town of Dongxing in Guangxi province.

- Huu Nghi border - connects the Vietnamese town of Dong Dang in Lang Son Province with Pinxiang and Nanning on the Chinese side. It is one of the busiest China-Vietnam border crossings, used when traveling overland from Hanoi to Nanning and Hong Kong.

To/from Laos

- Keo Nua Pass (also known as Cau Treo) - crossed when traveling from Lak Xao in Laos to the city of Vinh in Vietnam

- Lao Bao - usually used when traveling from Savannakhet in Laos to Hue in central Vietnam

TIP: Visas on arrival are **not** available for people entering Vietnam by land. If arriving by land, you need to obtain a Vietnam visa from your closest Vietnam Embassy before you set off. If you arrive by air and enter with a visa on arrival, there's no problem leaving by land.

DETAILS

Phones and SIM cards

Vietnam is very mobile-phone friendly, with cheap call rates, cheap phones and cheap data plans. Just about everyone has at least one mobile phone. In 2015, there were 123.8 million mobile phone subscribers in Vietnam. That's 141% of the population!

The main mobile phone service providers are:
- Mobifone (mobifone3g.com.vn)
- Vinaphone (vinaphone.com.vn); and
- the military-owned Viettel (www.vietteltelecom.vn - Vietnamese only).

TIP: You can buy SIM cards at any shop that sells mobile phones. They will sometimes ask to see your passport but it's not always necessary, as often the shop will register the new number themselves. If you are presented with an exercise book full of lists of numbers, you're being asked to choose your new cell/mobile phone number.

TIP: The easiest SIM card option is probably Mobifone's pay-as-you-go Mobicard. The VND50,000 (US$2.23) package includes a SIM card and the activation fee. You can buy top-up cards at street stalls and corner stores all over Vietnam. Just look for a "Mobi" sign and then indicate how much credit you'd like - VND20,000 VND50,000 or VND100,000. You'll get a small card with a scratch-off section containing a code that you input into your phone for instant credit. The Mobicard package allows you to send local and international texts as well as make local and international calls. The call and text rates are very low and are available on Mobifone's website in English.

Just about everyone has a mobile phone

Unlike in other countries, there are no cheap cell phone packages designed for short-term visitors. However, a basic phone can be purchased for about US$15 at any mobile phone store.

New telephone area codes began being phased in across Vietnam in 2015, changing the Hanoi area code to 024 from 04 and the Ho Chi Minh City area code to 028 from 08. However, the old telephone area codes will continue to work until March 1, 2017. The new area codes are used throughout this book.

TIP: When using a mobile/cell phone, you need to add the area code of the location you're calling, so the emergency police number would be 024-113 if you were calling from a mobile phone in Hanoi and 028-113 if you were calling from Ho Chi Minh City. This applies even if you are calling a Ho Chi Minh City phone number from a cell phone while you're in Ho Chi Minh City. Without the area code, you'll just get an annoying message in Vietnamese saying the number you dialed is not valid.

TIP: If you're traveling with a smart phone, ask the person in the mobile phone shop to set you up with a cheap data package. You can often get 1GB of data for as little as VND50,000 but these deals are usually only advertised in Vietnamese. In most cases, you have to enter a code on your phone to activate the cheap data deals, which is why you'll probably need assistance.

Money

The Vietnamese currency is the dong. Get used to saying it before you go. The Vietnamese pronunciation is "dom," which is not so snigger-worthy.

In Vietnam, you will be a millionaire. It can be a great feeling, walking down the street with an enormous wad of cash secreted somewhere on your personage. But it can also be slightly stressful because you don't want to be a victim of a multi-million dong snatch and grab - and it can be difficult to conceal US$300 once it's converted into VND6.75 million, a veritable brick of cash.

> TIP: The official currency rate is set by the government and rarely changes. When it does, it's usually only a minimal increase or decrease. For the latest rates, check www.xe.com/ucc.

> TIP: Vietnam dong can't be changed outside of Vietnam, so remember to change your dong to another more widely used currency before you leave the country.

> TIP: The foreign exchange counters at the major airports are government-owned and therefore offer the official exchange rate. You're not going to get a substantially better deal anywhere else, so make things easier on yourself and just use the airport currency exchange services.

> TIP: Be aware that taxi drivers, especially in the mornings, often don't have a lot of change. If you only have VND500,000 or VND200,000 notes, the driver may tell you he can't change it (and he might even be telling the truth). Try to make sure you have small notes of VND100,000 or less when taking a taxi anywhere. You might be able to change a bigger note at a shop or at the front desk of your

hotel, but don't count on it.

TIP: The no-change situation often happens at shops as well. So if a shop girl suddenly disappears down the street with a big note, she's probably asking other businesses to break the note for her so she can give you change. In one of those weird Vietnamese quirks, the more local you go, the more likely the vendor is to have a huge wad of cash to make change.

ATMs: Automatic teller machines are widely available in Vietnam, even in rural areas.

TIP: Local bank ATMs will only let you withdraw VND2 million to VND3 million at a time. This can be a pain because most international banks will ping you an international withdrawal fee for each transaction. The international banks - ANZ, Citibank, Commonwealth Bank and HSBC - will let you withdraw more per transaction, from VND4 million to VND10 million. Expect to be charged a transaction fee for using the ATM, as well as an international withdrawal fee by your bank. At the time of publication, four Commonwealth Bank ATMs in Ho Chi Minh City's backpacker district were not charging international withdrawal fees.

Electricity

Vietnam's power supply is 220/240 volts, 50Hz. The round two-pin plugs are the most common and adaptors are available in some supermarkets and electrical stores in Vietnam.

Appliances from Australia, the UK and most of Europe will operate in Vietnam as long as you have an adaptor to plug it into the socket.

Vietnam uses round two-prong electricity plugs

TIP: If you're coming from the US, where everything runs on 120 volts, before plugging anything into the wall, check to see what voltage range the device can handle. If you can find something that reads "input 100-240 volts", then it will work (or at least not explode) in Vietnam. If the device's transformer can't handle 240 volts, you'll need a voltage converter to operate it in Vietnam.

TIP: Unlike in Australia, the electrical sockets do not have an on-off switch. You just plug your appliance in and it's live, unplug it to turn it off.

Internet accessibility

Free wifi is available just about everywhere in Vietnam, from tiny 7-11-type convenience stores, fast food outlets, bars, cafes to hotels -- even in supermarkets! Just ask for the password and you'll be online instantly. (The word password is the same in English and in Vietnamese.)

TIP: If you're traveling with a smart phone, you can turn it into a wifi hotspot. On Android devices, you can do this through the "wireless & networks" section of the settings menu. On an iPhone, you go through "settings" to "personal hotspot" and your phone will talk you through the setup. This is a relatively cheap option if you've bought a local 3G enabled SIM card for your phone.

TIP: A 3G dongle (also known as an USB dongle) can get you online quickly and relatively cheaply in most areas of Vietnam. Dongles can be bought at mobile phone shops and charged with credit in the same way as mobile phones, by purchasing mobile phone credit and then inputting the code.

Shop & Go is just one chain of 24-hour convenience stores

TIP: A sign saying "wifi free" actually means "free wifi" because in Vietnamese the adjective comes after the noun. Don't be misled by the literal translation!

Facebook access

Facebook is regularly blocked by the government, although there are easy workarounds, which change as the government changes its tactics.

> TIP: Googling "Facebook blocked in Vietnam" will usually lead you to the latest workaround, which is often as simple as changing your computer's DNS code. And if you don't know how to do that, Google will have the answer as well!

Disability access

There isn't really any disability access in Vietnam. A 2011 government review of disability access to public transport and public buildings found "ease of access only exists in 22.6% of medical institutions, 20.8% of educational buildings and 13.2% of exhibitions," according to a *VietNews* report. The news report said even wheelchair ramps, where they existed, were often too steep or had no handrails or barriers. Throughout Vietnam, bus stops, letterboxes, automated teller machines and ticket selling booths are usually not wheelchair accessible.

Another significant obstacle to those in wheelchairs is the lack of useable sidewalks/footpaths. In most built-up areas, footpaths are used for parking motorbikes, running cafes, playing Chinese checkers and for stalls selling food, drinks, newspapers and lottery tickets.

A lucky ticket from the city of Can Tho in the Mekong Delta

While there are wheelchair-bound people in Vietnam, they seem to get around right in the middle of the traffic, either pushed by a family member or by propelling themselves with a pump-action steering wheel setup.

Ho Chi Minh City's Central Business District is ok for prams and wheelchairs

Vaccinations

The U.S. Centers for Disease Control and Prevention (CDC) recommends:

- Typhoid
- Hepatitis A
- Hepatitis B
- Japanese Encephalitis (if planning on visiting rural areas where there's a JE outbreak)
- Rabies (recommended for those planning to spend a lot of time outdoors engaging in activities such as hiking or cycling)

The CDC also recommends all routine vaccinations should be up to date before visiting Vietnam.

Dengue fever is prevalent in Vietnam. Take care at dawn and dusk when the *Aedes aegypti* mosquito is active, although the nasty little suckers bite at any time during the day. I ended up in an isolation ward in an expat hospital in Ho Chi Minh City with dengue in 2009. I was five months pregnant at the time and as you probably know, being pregnant suppresses your immune system and leaves you vulnerable to the nastier side of illness and infection. We all survived dengue without any long-lasting effects (my husband had it at the same time and the doctors suspect the same mosquito was responsible), but it was a worrying and very miserable few weeks for all of us. Dengue can be fatal in some cases, and I was very glad to be under close medical supervision for the worst of my bout.

Some parts of rural Vietnam are also considered malaria areas and tuberculosis is also still a problem. Discuss anti-malaria options and TB vaccinations with your travel doctor if you are planning on visiting or living in a rural area, especially if you have kids.

TIP: Check online for more medical advice specific to Vietnam.http://wwwnc.cdc.gov/travel/destinations/traveler/none/vietnam and http://www.smartraveller.gov.au/zw-cgi/view/Advice/Vietnam

Crossing the road

Motorbike traffic in Vietnam operates on the same principle as a school of fish. The traffic just flows around obstacles. So if you're that obstacle, the traffic should flow around you.

Motorbikes rule the roads in Vietnam

Getting stuck in the middle of the flow of traffic is scary, especially if you've got children with you, but just remember the school of fish principle. Whatever you do, don't panic and make a run for it. If you are still, motorbikes can go around. The people on the motorbikes have a vested interest in not hitting you, so try to make it easy for them to avoid you by being predictable. Walk slowly, watching the oncoming traffic and trying to make eye contact with everyone heading towards you (in case they're texting or talking to their mate sitting behind them). Wave one arm above your head to make sure people have noticed you. The waving will probably make you feel like a twit but it is effective — and that's coming from someone who's ridden a motorbike in heavy traffic in Vietnam. There's a lot going on; when you're driving you're not always looking in front of you!

> TIP: My school of fish theory only applies to motorbikes. Trucks and buses are the kings of the road. They won't try to go around. Do your very best not to get in front of them.

To cross the road, stand at the curb and look both ways, then look again. Don't wait for a gap in the traffic; you'll be stuck there til

46

you're a pensioner. Look for a lighter spot in the traffic. When you see it, step off the curb and walk slowly through the light spot, looking for the next light spot. Just be slow and steady and you should get to the other side in one piece.

> TIP: The easiest way for beginners to cross the road is to wait for a local to cross, and walk beside them. They will think your fear is hilarious, and they will usually try to make sure you survive the crossing.

CULTURAL REMINDERS

Politics

Vietnam is a one-party state and only one political party, the Communist Party of Vietnam, is allowed. There is no opposition party. People have been thrown in jail for posting comments on offshore websites promoting the concept of a multi-party democracy. Bloggers have also been imprisoned for writing about the issue.

Most Vietnamese people rarely discuss politics, except on the most superficial level. This is usually because they think there's not much point in talking about things that can't be changed.

It's best to avoid publicly discussing domestic politics while in Vietnam. By all means, criticize your own government and its policies but steer clear of saying anything that could be taken as disparaging the Vietnamese government, current or former leaders, the political system, the one-party system, the Communist Party of Vietnam or communism generally.

> TIP: If you are interested in the local political scene and want to ask questions of the locals, really monitor their responses carefully. If they're not saying anything of substance, they're politely trying to tell you to drop the subject. Don't keep pushing for information - you could end up causing trouble for the person you're talking to. After all, who knows who could be listening? Safe topics for conversation in Vietnam are sports, especially the European Championship and, of course, food.

Religion

Religious practices were restricted after the Communist victory in Vietnam in April 1975. Many religious buildings, including some Catholic-run schools and hospitals, were destroyed or reclaimed by the state.

Perhaps as a bit of a hangover from the restrictions during the strict Communist regime, many Vietnamese people still identify themselves as having no religion. (Party members are still not supposed to have a religion.) However, many Vietnamese regularly visit Buddhist pagodas and have an ancestor altar in their homes.

TIP: When visiting a temple, don't walk across the prayer mats, even when they're vacant. Also don't walk between people praying and the Buddha statue or whatever they're praying to. It's usually OK to take photos in temples, as long as you don't get right in people's faces.

A golden Buddha statue

Most businesses also have a little "good luck" shrine, with statuettes of Buddha, the god of luck and the god of earth.

No one is quite sure what currency they use in the afterlife, so most people send a mix of fake US dollars, Euros and dong.

Most homes in Vietnam will have a small shrine dedicated to the family's ancestors. Ancestor worship is not a religious practice but a Chinese-influenced belief that one's ancestors exist in another realm, able to send good luck and prosperity to their living descendants ... if the mood strikes them. Family shrines usually include photographs of the departed, fresh flowers, incense, and small offerings of fruit, rice wine, coffee and cigarettes. People can "send" worldly goods to their ancestors by burning paper items such as houses, motorbikes or hell money. The belief is that if you look after your ancestors, they will reciprocate by looking after you.

A temple attendant burns some hell money

The Vietnamese government's attitude towards religion is much more tolerant now than it was in the past and "freedom of belief and of religion" is enshrined in the constitution. However, as recently as 2014, at least 20 religious leaders and practitioners were arrested on charges of participating in independent religious groups not approved by the government. In 2013, several people were sentenced to between two and 22 years imprisonment for practicing banned religions, participating in protests and "undermining national unity".

A ceremony at a Buddhist temple

According to Human Rights Watch's 2015 World Report, the government targets unsanctioned religious groups, including unrecognized branches of the Cao Dai church, the Hoa Hao Buddhist church, independent Protestant and Catholic house churches, Khmer Krom Buddhist temples and the Unified Buddhist Church of Vietnam. Catholic priests and Montagnard Christians have also been affected by Vietnam's religious restrictions.

There are a several mosques and Hindu temples in Vietnam. In the Mekong Delta there's a local religion called Cao Dai, which reportedly has up to two million followers, mostly around the Cao Dai "Holy See" in Tay Ninh, northwest of Ho Chi Minh City.

Hue Nghiem Temple in Ho Chi Minh City's District 2

There are a number of churches in Hanoi and Ho Chi Minh City that have services in English, and Shabbat services are conducted in Ho Chi Minh City.

Hanoi

Hanoi International Fellowship meets at the Intercontinental Hanoi Westlake Hotel Grand Ballroom, A Nghi Tam Street, Tay Ho, Hanoi, at 10.30 am on Sundays. www.hifvn.org

Hanoi Cua Bac Church at No. 56, Phan Dinh Phung. The English service is at 10 am.

Hanoi International Church Service at the Hanoi Club, 76 Yen Phu.

Meets every Sunday at 10.30 am. www.hicvn.org

Ho Chi Minh City

International Christian Fellowship, Hoa Hung Church (Methodist), 625D Cach Mang Thang Tam Street, District 10. Sunday service in English, 10.30 am.

Notre Dame Cathedral, Dong Khoi Street, District 1, holds a Roman Catholic mass in English every Sunday at 9.30 am.

Notre Dame Cathedral, HCMC

Dai Chung Vien Thanh Giuse, 6 Ton Duc Thang St, District 1. Mass in English on Saturdays at 6 pm.

Hội Thánh Tin Lành Việt Nam (Miền Nam) (Saigon Evangelical Church) 155 Trần Hưng Đạo, has an English translation at the 8.30 am service on Sundays. Sit in the first three rows and you'll be given headphones.

Shabbat services are conducted every week at the Chabard of Vietnam, 5A Nguyen Dinh Chieu St, District 1. Meals are served after the services at the Chabard, Vietnam's only kosher restaurant.

Nha Tho Tan Dinh (Tan Dinh Church) in Ho Chi Minh City

Kon Tum's amazing wooden church

Daily Life

There are a few parts of daily Vietnamese life that seem strange to outsiders.

There is a completely different concept of privacy in Vietnam, probably closely linked to the practicalities of multi-generational dwellings. With so many people living in the one house, it's uncommon for a child -- or an adult -- to have a bedroom of their own. In many cases, the entire family sleeps in the same room and shares one bathroom. And so there is not much privacy at all.

Daily life in Vietnam usually revolves around food. In a multi-generational household, there is usually at least one woman -- a maid, an auntie or a grandmother -- whose role is to feed, or organize the feeding of, the family. This hardworking woman could go to the market up to three times a day to get supplies. Even though most families now have a refrigerator, the overriding belief is that fresh is best when it comes to meat, fish, seafood and produce.

This endless cycle of shopping, cooking and eating is supplemented, or enhanced, by eating out and drinking (*đi nhau*).

Chinese-influenced folklore still plays a major role in daily life, in the form of ancestor worship and paying homage to the gods -- the God of Earth, the God of Luck and the kitchen gods (made universally famous by an Amy Tan novel).

As mentioned in the previous section, most households have a small shrine dedicated to the God of Earth and the God of Luck. The kitchen gods don't have their own shrine but they are still considered important. Or at least, important enough to try to appease them once a year.

On the 23rd day of the 12th month of the lunar calendar, the kitchen god rides a goldfish to heaven to report on the household happenings of the past year.

It takes a week for *Ông Táo,* the kitchen god, to travel to heaven, file his findings with the Jade Emperor (*Ngọc Hoàng*), then return to his kitchen.

To ensure a good report, on the day he's due to depart, families pile *Ông Táo's* altar, which most kitchens used to have, with fruit and candy. People also release carp into the nearest river, to help the kitchen god get to heaven quickly, and in a good mood. All these special treats for *Ông Táo* are not considered bribery ... but it comes pretty close. For after *Ông Táo* reports, the Jade Emperor decides whether to send the family good or bad luck for the year ahead.

Another Vietnamese tradition that can seem strange to outsiders is the death anniversary "party".

The party is an annual gathering of the family, on the anniversary of someone's death, to honor the deceased and appease their spirit, which is hanging out in another realm, supposedly able to influence the fortunes of those still living in the mortal domain. It's usually the father's parents and grandparents who are honored this way. The mother's ancestors are supposed to be honored by their sons and their families.

In the more pious families, death anniversary parties involve tributes and prayers, sometimes at home, sometimes at a pagoda, dedicated to the departed. In other families, death anniversaries are riotous drunken affairs that last well into the night.

Whether a death anniversary party is virtuous or debauched, they're a bit different to a funeral party, which shares some characteristics of the European wake.

Like a wake, a funeral party involves keeping watch over the body of the deceased, which is usually cased in a flower-covered coffin in the family's living room. The "party" is usually conducted next to the living room, often in a marquee that is set up in the street.

During the party, which can last for three days, the family makes a lot of noise to encourage the spirit of the deceased to leave. Crying or acting sad in any way is frowned upon, as it could worry the spirit and keep it close to the family when it should be moving on to the next realm. The noise can take the form of bad karaoke or an out-of-tune brass band playing numbers that sound like the worst school band in the history of the world.

A funeral marquee being set up, with the multicolored funeral flag

TIP: Don't take photos of funeral processions, funeral parties or coffin-makers. Funerals are easy to identify because everyone is wearing white headbands or fully-clothed in white and there's usually a multicolored square funeral flag flying nearby. As fascinating as this tradition is, it's best to refrain from taking photos and just nod respectfully to anyone whose eye you might catch as you pass by. If you are invited to join the "party", feel free to do so.

Another slightly odd Vietnamese tradition is the professional ear-cleaning service offered at barber shops.

The telltale sign that a barber shop offers this service is a lamp, one of the most vital pieces of equipment, along with a frightening array of brushes, picks and scrapers.

One of my Vietnamese friends gets his ears cleaned once a week because he suffers from itchy ears. He says it feels like a massage inside his head and he finds it very relaxing. However, Westerners I know who have submitted their ears for cleaning say the process can be quite painful.

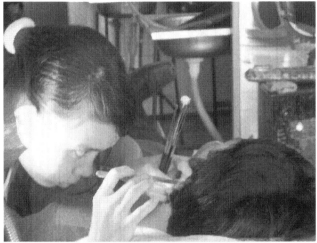

A professional ear cleaner at work

TIP: This obsession with clean ears is one of the reasons why some Vietnamese men have an outlandishly long fingernail on their pinkie. For some, a grow-your-own-Q-Tip is a way to save money on ear-cleaning fees. For other men, the super-long fingernail is a sign that the bearer is not a manual labourer.

Tet

Tết is the most important celebration in Vietnam. Most businesses shut down for a week or longer, depending on how many public holidays are declared.

The date of *Tết* varies from year to year, depending on the lunar calendar. Employees receive a 13th month bonus just before the *Tết* holiday, which marks the end of the old lunar year and the start of a new.

`Happy new year' street decorations from 2013

In preparation for the new year, houses are thoroughly cleaned and sometimes renovated. All over the country people are cleaning, painting, cooking and shopping for new things. The crush in the stores is incredible. Everyone goes home for *Tết* and getting bus, train tickets or air tickets for the peak traveling days is a very competitive business.

Ho Chi Minh City and Hanoi turn into ghost towns during the holiday. Most people travel to their hometowns for intensive rounds of visiting friends and family members and pagodas.

On the first day of the Lunar New Year, Vietnamese families spend time together, visiting their local temple and receiving guests. The first visitor to cross the threshold should bring good luck.

> TIP: Some Vietnamese believe foreigners bring good luck, some believe they don't. So foreigners living in Vietnam should not visit anyone on the first two or three days of *Tết* unless specifically invited.

At *Tết*, children are given *lì xì*, red envelopes containing cash, known as lucky money. When employees return to work after the *Tết* holiday, they usually also get a small amount of *lì xì*. Lucky money should be crisp new notes to herald in the crisp new Lunar New Year.

Tết hampers, usually given by businesses to clients, can include whiskey, Danish butter cookies, crackers and what the Vietnamese translate into English as "jam", which is actually candied dried fruit. (My favourite is the candied dried coconut. Also, I've never actually seen anyone eat a Danish butter cookie!)

Tết snacks

Special *Tết* food is prepared, including a glutinous rice and meat roll called *bánh tét* in the south and *bánh chưng* in the north. The object of the hampers and the furious pre- *Tết* cooking and shopping is to give everyone, even the ever-dedicated and hardworking housewives, a break, so they can start the new year feeling relaxed, carefree and, above all, lucky.

No cleaning is undertaken on the first day of *Tết*. (You don't want to sweep away your good luck!) Traditionally, no one cooks either. After all that cleaning, everyone needs a rest.

Etiquette

Vietnamese people seem to be fairly tolerant of foreigners and don't really expect non-Vietnamese to know the customs and practices of Vietnamese life.

However, it's much better to make an effort to be polite than offend people for some minor breach of etiquette. So here's a random selection of day-to-day etiquette tips I've picked up over the years.

> TIP: Accept business cards (or name cards) with both hands. Look at the text on both sides before putting it somewhere prominent. Only put it away in a pocket, wallet or handbag when the meeting or event is over.

> TIP: In the same manner, when you want to show respect, accept or present documents or money with both hands. If the item is too small to fit in two hands, offer it one hand, with the other hand supporting the offered arm.

> TIP: A common greeting in Vietnam when visiting someone's house, especially around meal times, is *"Ăn cơm chưa?"* – literally 'have you eaten rice yet' but the meaning is "have you eaten yet?" Before answering honestly, take a moment to assess the situation. This is a traditional greeting that is now used just to be polite. If you say you haven't eaten, the host is obliged to feed you. The polite response is to say "yes, I have eaten" *(Dạ. Ăn cơm rồi.)* Even if you haven't eaten, it's best to say you have, to respond to the polite question with an appropriately polite response. (Unless you are really hungry, of course.)

> TIP: As a general rule, showing respect to your elders is important (usually by asking after their health). In this vein, in a social setting, try not to disagree with an older person who is giving you advice.

> TIP: When eating with Vietnamese people, you indicate you've finished eating by leaving something in your bowl to show you just can't fit anymore in. If you empty your bowl,

someone will fill it up again! Like any rule, there are always exceptions. In this case, devout Buddhists don't follow this practice because they don't like to waste anything.

TIP: At restaurants and cafes, iced green or jasmine tea is usually free once you order something. Wet napkins wrapped in plastic (which are sometime refrigerated), however, are not free. They usually cost VND2,000 or VND3,000 per napkin and the charge will be added to your bill. This is not some foreigner-scam - it's common practice in Vietnam. So when you ask for the bill and the waiter stands there staring at the mess on the table for a bit, he or she is counting the number of napkins you've used.

TIP: At more local places, what you order isn't necessarily recorded anywhere. Neither are empty bottles or plates cleared by the wait staff. When you call for the bill, the wait staff will count the empty plates and bottles in order to add up the bill. Again, this explains the strange occurrence of a waiter or waitress checking the mess on -- and under -- the table after you've called for the bill.

TIP: Be aware that Western standards of politeness are not universal. In Vietnam it's not rude to stare, so people stare. It can be a bit confronting to be sitting somewhere having a drink surrounded by a crowd of people staring at you.

TIP: It's also not rude to pick your nose or squeeze pimples in public in Vietnam. If it offends you, look away.

TIP: Vietnamese people engage in a lot of same-sex touching. It's not sexual or even homosexual. A Western man can get a bit of a surprise the first time a colleague drapes his hand over his upper thigh. It's a sign of friendship, nothing more. And the Westerner should feel honored that the other guy feels comfortable enough to do this. I found it fascinating to watch how touchy-feely guys got with each other in the office. (I didn't notice it so much among women in the office, but maybe it was because I was too busy watching the guys.) Vietnamese girls do snuggle up to each other and lean against each other when they walk around. Be very careful not to breach the sex divide. Men and women don't touch in public. If you are working with Vietnamese people, try not to touch someone of the opposite sex. If you forget and give someone a friendly tap on the shoulder, it's not wildly offensive but it could make the person feel very uncomfortable, or consider it a come-on.

TIP: There's an old superstition, still held by many of the older generation in Vietnam, that taking a photo of three people is bad luck, with the person in the middle of the photo likely to be struck down with the worst luck, usually in the form of death.

TIP: Be wary of "inviting". The custom in Vietnam is for the person who issues the invitation to pick up the bill. If someone has invited you out for dinner or a drink, they will pay. (Don't argue, reciprocate another time.) They will probably phrase it like this "I invite you to xxx." That means they'll pay. It can be an expensive lesson to ask if anyone's interested in an after-work drink, then find you're expected to pick up the tab for the entire party at the end of the night. Especially if your colleagues have been ordering top-shelf stuff!

TIP: People will ask your age. This is because there is no "you" or "I" in Vietnamese. The relationship determines the pronouns used. So if I am younger than the person I'm talking to, I refer to myself as *em* (younger sister). If I am older than the person I'm talking to, I refer to myself as *chị* (older sister). People ask your age so they can work out whether to call you older brother, younger brother, younger sister, older sister, auntie, uncle who's younger than my father, uncle who's older than my father or even grandma or grandpa. There are numerous permutations. Plus, Vietnamese people are pretty curious and may really want to know how old you are.

TIP: Expect other personal questions, such as: How many beers can you drink? How many bowls of rice can you eat?

How much do you weigh? How much money do you have? Are you married? (The polite response is "not yet" rather than no, if that's the case.) Do you have children? (Again, "not yet" is an acceptable response. "No" is difficult to comprehend to Vietnamese, who are very family-oriented.) It's probably good to prepare a response to the other standards questions: How do you feel about Vietnam? And: How do you feel about Vietnamese food?

TIP: Take your shoes off before entering a temple, someone's home or any business that has shoes piled up in front of the door.

Personal space and queuing

Vietnamese people have a much smaller concept of personal space than most Westerners. This can make some people feel edgy, especially when the personal space evaporates completely, leaving someone actually touching you. It also creates a cultural divide when it comes to queuing.

Vietnamese people generally don't queue. Instead, everyone pushes forward, voicing their requests and waving pieces of paper and/or money in a bid to get attention.

TIP: Experience has taught me that waiting patiently just behind the mob usually doesn't get a result. In a non-queuing situation, it helps to have a bit of height so you can look over the heads of the non-queuers to make eye contact with the person who is serving. Pulling a helpless pleading face should prompt the serving person to deal with you ... eventually. If you don't have the height, there's nothing for it, you'll just have to wade in and get to the front to get attention.

TIP: When Vietnamese people do queue, such as at the supermarket or the airport, the space between queuers is a lot smaller than most Westerners are used to. If you leave a normal-to-you sized gap, sometimes Vietnamese people will cut in front of you ... because they don't realize you're actually queuing. People will even try to close the gap by pushing you gently with their trolley, just to let you know there's space in front of you. Try not to lose it when this happens, people are *probably* not being rude or trying to push in, it's just one of those cultural differences.

Memories of the war

In the countries aligned with the "invading" side of the Vietnam War (known in Vietnam as the American War), the word Vietnam is still shorthand for the war that dominated the political landscape of the 1960s and 1970s. The Vietnam War looms large in the Western consciousness and many Americans and Australians worry about how they will be perceived, given their nation's involvement in the Vietnam War.

In Vietnam, however, not much thought is given to the last war. The war ended 40 years ago and the average age of the population is 29. The younger generations have their eyes on the future and all the possibilities it holds. They don't really know much about the war because the older people who do remember the war are usually reluctant to talk about it and the Vietnamese school curriculum makes only passing reference to the American War.

Westerners are no longer regarded as former invaders. Instead, they're viewed more as interesting, slightly odd curiosities who bring welcome tourist dollars into Vietnam.

The main relic of the Vietnam/American War is the ongoing effects of dioxin, the herbicide known as Agent Orange that American forces used as a defoliant across vast swathes of central and southern Vietnam. Agent Orange is believed to have caused birth defects, neurological disorders, intellectual disabilities, cancer and many other health problems. Estimates for the number of Vietnamese people who suffer health problems related to exposure to dioxins range from 1 million to 3 million. The U.S. didn't help the dioxin cleanup efforts in Vietnam until 2012, when a joint U.S.-Vietnam project to decontaminate soil at Danang Airport, where Agent Orange was stored during the war, began.

Tipping

Tipping is not required and is not such a common practice in Vietnam. In touristy and high-end areas, staff may expect you to tip if they think you're American and used to tipping.

> TIP: Many hotels and restaurants add a 5% service charge to the bill. I don't tip when I see the service charge on the bill, even though I'm not convinced the service staff actually get the money.

> TIP: Some dodgy massage places operate a tipping scam, which involves holding customers for ransom after their massage until they pay a tip. Sometimes the bill states quite openly that you won't be allowed to leave the premises until you tip your masseuse. Try to avoid getting sucked into the scam by asking about their tipping policy at reception.

Toilets

Most airports, bars, cafes and restaurants in Vietnam have Western-style toilets.

You'll probably only have to deal with a squat toilet if you travel outside the major cities and/or visit a very local kind of tourist attraction.

> TIP: Most toilets in Vietnam come with a butt-hose. They can be your best friend or your worst enemy. If you get a dose of the squirts, use the butt-hose instead of toilet paper to preserve your butt-skin. Be warned - there is a bit of a knack to the butt-hose (and to drying off afterwards).

The rest stops on bus trips often have squat toilets. On the trains, most carriages will have a squat toilet in the restroom at one end of each carriage and a Western-style toilet in the rest room at the other end.

Squat toilets are pretty easy to use. If you are wearing long pants, roll them up before stepping onto the toilet. (Some toilets are on a pedestal, making the process seem very regal.) If there is a hood-type thing on one end of the squat toilet, that's the front. Keep the bottom of your pants off the floor and lower the top of the pants, squat down, holding on to the wall if you feel unsteady and then rest yourself on the back of your calves and do your business.

> TIP: If you have sunglasses perched on top of your head, don't look down into the toilet to check your aim because they will fall off and you'll have to fish them out. *And yes, I am speaking from experience here.*

> TIP: Not all toilets, or even all Western-style toilets, will have toilet paper. It's a good idea to carry a small packet of tissues, just in case. A lot of Western-style toilets aren't capable of flushing toilet paper. If there is a small rubbish bin in the toilet cubicle, throw the used toilet paper in there.

LANGUAGE

Vietnamese, classified as a tonal Mon-Khmer language, is the dominant language. The level of English is low compared to many other countries around the world, although most service staff in the heavily-touristed areas can speak varying degrees of English. Some older Vietnamese people speak French and/or Russian.

English is taught in schools and many young people continue studying the language after they graduate. These people are often keen to practice their English. However, there are many Vietnamese people who are quite shy about their English abilities and often choose not to speak rather than display their rudimentary grasp of the language.

TIP: Be patient with people with basic English: choose simple words, speak slowly and wait for them to process what you've just said. Repeating what you've said louder won't help, neither will launching into a long-winded secondary question designed to explain the first.

TIP: The English taught in schools focuses on reading and writing skills. As a result, some people's spoken English can be difficult to understand. After a while you will begin to see some patterns -- the final consonants of words often disappear and people use a robotic nasal monotone. This is because the final consonants are not pronounced in Vietnamese. Also, with six tones in their native language, people use the "no-tone" tone when speaking non-tonal English, and this no tone can be quite nasal. Vietnamese words are all one syllable long, so there is no need for the stresses and emphases used in multisyllabic English words. When every syllable gets the same emphasis, English can be a little difficult to understand. So be patient with strange English -- it's not an easy language to learn and their odd English is going to be much better than your Vietnamese.

A lotus lamp in a Buddhist temple

If you want to learn Vietnamese, there are many options, including private tutors, who usually advertise in expat magazines and on websites such as TNH (previously *The New Hanoian*) and www.expat-blog.com. There are also a variety of language classes available in the main cities.

> TIP: The English word "yum" sounds like the Vietnamese word for "horny". Be careful how you compliment delicious food. Things could get lost in translation!

Vietnamese language schools

Hanoi

The University of Social Sciences and Humanities-Hanoi
B7 Bis, Tran Dai Nghia Street, Bách Khoa, Hanoi
Tel: (+84-24) 3858 3798
ussh.vnu.edu.vn/en/for-foreign-students/vietnamese-language-courses-for-international-students

Hidden Hanoi
147 Nghi Tam Road, Tay Ho, Hanoi
Tel: (+84) (0) 912 254 045
www.hiddenhanoi.com.vn/languageschool

LESH English Center
422 Le Duan Alley, Dong Da
Tel: (+84) (0) 915 118 608

Mai's Professional Translation and Vietnamese Teaching Center
No.14, Lane.107, Tho Quan Alley, Kham Thien, Dong Da
Tel: (+84) (0) 974 020 552

Viettonkin Center for Education and Training
No 23, Hoang Nhu Tiep, Gia Lam
Tel: (+84) (0) 438 728 518

Ho Chi Minh City

University of Social Sciences and Humanities - Ho Chi Minh City.
10-12 Dinh Tien Hoang, District 1
Tel: (+84-28) 3822 5009
en.hcmussh.edu.vn

Vietnamese Language Garden
47/11/9 Quốc Hương, Thảo Điền Ward, District 2
Tel: (+84) (0) 916 670 771
www.vietnameselanguagegarden.vn

VLS Saigon
4th floor, CMARD 2, 45 Dien Tien Hoang, District 1
Tel: (+84-28) 3910 0168
vlstudies.com

VNC Vietnamese Language Training & Translation
37/54 Tran Dinh Xu, District 1
Tel: (+84-28) 6678 0914
www.vnccentre.com

Basic Vietnamese Phrases

Vietnamese is a bugger of a language to learn. There are six tones
and nine extra vowels. There's no J and there are two different types
of D (D and Đ). And then there are the regional accents, which make
one of the Vietnamese Ds (the D without the cross) sound like Z in
the north and Y in the south. G sometimes gets a Y sound and in the
south, V also sometimes gets a Y sound. The only thing that would
make Vietnamese more difficult to learn was if the ancient
characters, *chữ nôm*, were still in use.

With all this in mind, the following phrases may or may not be
understood if you say them aloud. However, they definitely will be
understood if you bring along the printed text and point (*such* a

71

useful form of communication), because Vietnam has a literacy rate of about 93%, which is high for a developing economy.

> TIP: In my (very food-centric) opinion, *em oi* is the most important Vietnamese phrase. This is Vietnamese for "hey you" and it's what's needed to summon waiters and waitresses who may be deeply involved in a conversation about the latest Vietnam Idol and so unaware that you need another round of beers or another plate of soft-shelled crab.

> The *em* in *em oi* means younger brother or sister, so if you are trying to catch the attention of a server who's older than you, you should use *anh oi* (hey older brother) or *chị oi* (hey older sister). The *oi* part of *em oi* is also a lot more polite than plain old "hey" in English.

Here are some helpful basic phrases.

Hello - *xin chào*
Goodbye - *tạm biệt*
Please - *làm ơn*
Thank you - *cảm ơn*
You're welcome - *không có chi*
Sorry/excuse me - *xin lỗi*
How much (does that cost)? *Bao nhiêu tiền* or simply *bao nhiêu*
Too expensive - *mắc quá*
Where - *ở đâu*
Where is the toilet? *Toilet ở đâu?*
Where is the hospital? - *Bệnh viện ở đâu?*
Where is a doctor? - *Bác sĩ ở đâu?*
Where is a pharmacy? - *Nhà thuốc ở đâu?*
Where is a hotel? - *Khách sạn ở đâu?*
Where is a wet market? - *Chợ ở đâu?*
Where is a supermarket? - *Siêu thị ở đâu?*
Where is the police station? - *Công An phư ờng ở đâu?*
Where is the post office? - *Bưu Điện ở đâu?*
I am sick - *Tôi bị bệnh*
I am lost - *Tôi bị lạc Đường*

Help me - *giúp tôi*
No - *không*
Yes - *dạ (sounds a lot like the German ja)*

TIP: There are also some uniquely Vietnamese hand gestures. The most common one is the hand-waggle (almost like a version of jazz hands), with the hands held under the ears, palms forwards and rotated a few times. Like the Indian head-bobble, the Vietnamese hand-waggle has a range of meanings, depending on the circumstances. A double hand-waggle can mean anything from "I don't know" to "who knows" to a flat-out "no" or "not available". A single hand-waggle can be a question, such as "where?"

TIP: Other universal food-related hand gestures also work in Vietnam. To call for the bill, sign an imaginary bill in the air. To ask for the menu, hold your palms together and then open them up like a book. Pointing to your watch (or an imaginary watch) means "how long" and pointing to something (such as a beer) and then holding up one finger means "one more" (with two fingers for "two more"). And, at the end of all this exhausting miming, remember to say "thank you". Everyone in Vietnam understands this English phrase.

Food phrases

Bring me (with an implied "please"): *em cho tôi:*

The menu - *menu*

A beer - *bia*

A cold beer - *một bia ướp lạnh*

Water - *nước* or *nước suối*

73

Cold/chilled water: *nước suối ướp lạnh*

Ice - *đá*

More beer - *thêm bia*

More ice - *thêm đá*

An iced coffee with milk - *Cà phê sữa đá*

An iced black coffee - *Cà phê đen đá*

With sugar: *có đường*

No sugar - *không đường*

A hot coffee with milk - *cà phê sữa nóng*

A hot black coffee - *cà phê đen nóng*

Vegetarian - *chay*

Dog meat* - *cầy, thịt cầy* or *thịt chó*

Salad - *xà lách* or *gỏi trộn*

Ice-cream - *kem*

French Fries - *khoai tây chiên*

Rice - *cơm*

A fork - *nia*

A spoon - *muỗng*

A knife - *dao*

Chopsticks - *đũa*

A glass - *ly*

I am hungry - *Tôi đói*

I am full - *Tôi no*

No chilli - *không ớt*

A little chilli - *ớt ít*

Spicy - *cay*

Not spicy - *không cay*

Kilo – kí lô

Gram - gờ ram

* I've included the word for dog meat NOT to recommend anyone order it, but to help people avoid confusing it with the word for vegetarian.

WHAT TO WEAR

Most Vietnamese people dress casually but conservatively. The local style is usually jeans or long pants and t-shirts with easy-to-slip-off shoes. Shorts and sleeveless t-shirts/singlets are considered the domain of old men.

Business attire is usually smart-casual or office-wear for women and business trousers/dress pants and a collared shirt for men. Some businessmen wear suits, particularly in Hanoi where there is a cooler season. In most cases, in the south, a suit usually isn't required.

Most Vietnamese women cover up completely during the day. Even when it's 33 degrees Celsius (91F), women will be driving motorbikes in the sun wearing a hoodie, a face mask, evening gloves, socks and even a huge wrap-around skirt over the top of everything.

Bare flesh is rarely seen during the daytime, not even at the beach. Be aware of this conservatism when you're packing -- short-shorts and spaghetti strapped tank tops aren't really appropriate unless you're at a Western-style high-end resort.

At night, some female bare flesh can be seen but, when combined with lots of makeup, it's usually an indication of a certain type of girl, if you know what I mean. Outside the main cities, people dress even more conservatively and visitors really should follow the lead of the locals.

> TIP: When visiting temples, especially, it's important that adults and teenagers have knees, shoulders and other saucy bits covered. Kids are OK in less conservative clothes but nothing too racy. Women can carry a scarf with them to wear over bare shoulders when visiting temples.

> TIP: Vietnamese regard "long" or "high" noses as beautiful. This refers to the bridge of your nose. Caucasians usually have an arch between their eyes, where their nose starts. Vietnamese people are flat here. Even if your nose has never been complimented before, in Vietnam it may be considered stunning. Accept nose compliments with a gracious smile.

WHAT LOCALS WEAR

Vietnam can seem to be a very laid-back country, with half the population never bothering to get out of their pajamas. In the markets and on the streets, many women wear stretchy patterned shirt-and-top sets that look like pajamas to Western eyes. But all is not as it seems ... they are not pajamas, even though some people sleep in them.

The most common form of pajama outfit is the *đồ bộ,* which is obviously very comfortable attire.

Doing a đồ bộ dance

Most young professional women wouldn't be caught dead wearing a *đồ bộ* in public. The outfits are considered somewhat working class, even peasant-ish. Grandmas, market ladies, wandering vendors and maids like to get around in *đồ bộ.* Women usually don a clean *đồ bộ* after a shower, and wear it round-the-clock until it's shower-time again. Some women wear a *đồ bộ* at home and change into "going out" clothes to leave the house.

Another pajama-like outfit is the *áo bà ba,* a silk tunic and pants set commonly worn in southern Vietnam. Nowadays, *áo bà ba* are mostly worn by the older generation.

Related to these pajama-like outfits is the *áo dài* (pronounced ow yay in the south and ow zay in the north), the Vietnamese national costume. First introduced in the imperial court of Nguyen Phuc Khoat in 1744, the *áo dài* has evolved over time into the current tight-fitting tunic over loose flowing silk pants..

A white *áo dài* is the uniform for high school girls throughout Vietnam. Some banks and hotels also have an *áo dài* as a uniform. Although the *áo dài* is mostly seen on women, there is a male version, which is looser than the female *áo dài*. Male *áo dài*, however, are usually only worn by grooms during a wedding photo shoot. For other formal occasions, Vietnamese men wear suits or business attire.

Girls posing in áo dài

TIP: Most of the uniformed men you see on the streets are parking attendants. They consider themselves security guards but their job is really to make sure no one steals the parked motorbikes they watch over. This "uniform" is pretty standard, featuring a blue shirt with epaulettes.

GETTING AROUND

The majority of Vietnam's population cannot afford cars and the cities and towns aren't really designed for walking, so motorbikes rule the streets.

Motorbike

I ride a motorbike in Vietnam but I only ventured out on my own after several months of being in the traffic on the back of a motorbike driven by a *xe ôm* (motorbike taxi) driver. There is some natural sense in how the traffic works in Vietnam, even if it may seem like utter chaos at first glance.

Xe om drivers usually wait for fares on street corners

After several years in Vietnam, I was quite surprised to discover there actually are road rules, although the rules are often regarded as merely "suggestions". The one rule that's followed by the majority of people is wearing a helmet on a motorbike, probably because this is a very obvious breach of the rules, which can result being stopped by the traffic police.

Motorbikes on Ha Tien beach

Helmets are compulsory but many people think they will damage kids' necks

Being pulled over by the police is going to cost you. In some cases, you will be issued with a ticket and your bike confiscated for a certain period of time. In other cases, the police officer will ask for a bribe in exchange for not issuing a ticket and taking your bike. Stay calm and be respectful, no matter what happens. Getting angry will only make the situation worse.

The other main road rules are:

- a maximum of two adults on a motorbike;

- the speed limit in city areas is 35 km/hour (unless otherwise posted) for motorbikes, 45 km/hour for cars; and

- the speed limit on the highway is 50 km/hour unless otherwise posted for motorbikes, and for cars the highway speed limit is 80km/hour unless otherwise posted.

A Vietnamese driver's license is required to drive legally in Vietnam, although many motorbike places will rent you a bike even if you don't have a license. Unlicensed driving used to be pretty much the norm among non-Vietnamese motorbike drivers but the police are now cracking down on the practice. If the police catch you driving without a license, you can be fined and the motorbike confiscated.

If you are involved in an accident when driving without a license, you won't be covered by insurance and you will also have to compensate the other party.

This compensation system means that it can be cheaper to compensate for a death than for an injury that results in a condition that requires life-long care. In the seconds before an accident, this fact may flash through a Vietnamese driver's mind and they may take actions to ensure the "cheaper" option of death occurs. Bear this in mind when you're on the roads.

TIP: When a traffic fatality occurs, the police usually arrive en masse and mark out the death scene in white paint. It's not cool to take photos of this.

TIP: International licenses have not been recognized in Vietnam in the past. The government has announced that they will recognize international licenses in the near future, but the details and start date of this recognition had not been announced at the time of publication.

A motorbike fixing station, found on just about every street corner

Motorbikes are real workhorses in Vietnam, conveying everything, including truck tires, toilets, kitchen sinks, queen-sized mattresses, computer hard drives, blocks of ice, crates of beer, live seafood in buckets with aerators, groceries, construction materials and panes of glass. Vietnamese people are so inventive; you never ever will have seen it all when it comes to things being carried on motorbikes.

A loaded-up motorbike

Train

The Reunification Express runs from Ho Chi Minh City to Hanoi. The full journey takes 33 hours. For timetables and fares, see www.seat61.com/Vietnam.htm.

The fares are quite reasonable, with a lower berth soft sleeper for the entire Ho Chi Minh City-Hanoi route setting you back VND1.7 million or about US$77. You could cut the cost of the trip by traveling on a hard or soft seat, or even in an uncomfortable-sounding hard sleeper (which is actually quite comfortable). The main difference between a soft sleeper and a hard sleeper is the number of beds in the cabin. There are four beds in a soft sleeper and six in a hard sleeper. There isn't really enough room to sit up in a hard sleeper, but maybe you won't need to.

Snack time in a soft seat on the train in Vietnam

Bus

Passenger buses are widely available throughout Vietnam, even to the remotest villages. You can book bus services through any travel agent and/or hotel or guesthouse.

Generally, tourists end up on coaches rather than the uber-local minibuses, which can be a bit crowded.

Vietnam has an extensive system of open tour buses. These are hop-on-hop-off services that can usually be booked at the last minute. The routes and the schedules are fixed and the fares are usually quite cheap.

Some tourist buses are very comfortable with wide plush seats. Some are not, with narrow seats and no toilet on board. It's a good idea to check exactly what you'll get when you book.

> TIP: Some bus drivers are a bit horn-happy, even on overnight sleeper routes. If you're planning to nap or sleep on a bus, ear plugs might be necessary.

Taxis

Taxis are available in most of Vietnam's larger towns. In the bigger cities, some taxis have doctored meters, which can spin like a slot machine. Generally, though, taxi drivers use the meters and the fares are relatively cheap. For example, a taxi from the airport to downtown Ho Chi Minh City costs around VND150,000 (US$7).

> TIP: Look for reputable taxi companies – Vinasun and Mai Linh in Ho Chi Minh City, and Hanoi Taxi and Mai Linh in Hanoi.

> TIP: Consider a taxi for medium-range trips. It can be a reasonable option, especially when you can just get in and go and not have to worry about timetables or booking seats or getting paper tickets delivered. There are set fees for many day trip destinations, which taxi company telephone operators are able to quote. Often the quote comes with a proviso that the excursion doesn't exceed a certain number of hours. For example, Mai Linh taxi company in Ho Chi Minh City quotes VND1.44 million (US$67) for a seven-hour day trip to the Cu Chi Tunnels. Taxi drivers often don't speak much English, so don't expect the driver to act as a tour guide.

Uber, GrabTaxi and GrabBike also operate in Vietnam.

ACCOMMODATION

Vietnam has a wide range of accommodation, from super-cheap backpacker hostels to fancy five star resorts.

Hotel booking sites are a great resource when it comes to researching short-term accommodation in Vietnam. I usually check www.asiarooms.com, www.agoda.com, www.hotelscombined.com and www.airbnb.com to get an idea of what's available in our budget. I then check whether the property I'm interested in has its own website to see whether the booking sites will actually deliver a discount.

> TIP: If you're staying several days in a location, you can often find cheaper-than-the-internet digs by walking into hotels and asking their rates in person. If you book one or two nights in advance, you can do this once you hit the

ground. I don't think this is a worthwhile tactic if you're traveling through Vietnam quickly, staying only one or two nights in each location.

All along the tourist trail there's cheap accommodation targeted at backpackers and upscale places for high-end travelers. There are also hotels that cater to domestic travelers and these places are often great value, especially if you're traveling with a family. They often offer family rooms with two or three queen-sized beds. However, these cheaper hotels are usually tall skinny buildings that don't have lifts, so bear that in mind when researching (and packing).

> TIP: Because Vietnamese people like rock hard beds and nylon sheets, these items are often standard in local-style hotels and guest houses. If you think you might have a problem with super-hard beds and/or synthetic sheets, ask to see a room before you check in.

Short-term serviced apartments are available in Ho Chi Minh City and Hanoi. Holiday apartments are not cheap by any means, and are very difficult to find outside of these two cities.

> TIP: Vietnam is pretty new to the homestay concept. Some homestays can be pretty basic, some can be wonderful experiences. Keep your expectations low and hopefully you'll be pleasantly surprised. The exception is in the Mekong Delta, where there are several upscale homestays providing an off-the-beaten track experience.

Government regulations require hotels and guest houses to record the passport details of all their guests. Some hotels ask to hold the passports, others will keep your passports for a short while and then return them. This is not a scam - all hotels need to do this. Just remember to retrieve your passports when you check out.

Check-in staff may also ask to see a couple's marriage certificate, although this is usually only requested when a Western man and an Asian woman check into the same room.

DINING

Ah, the food! It's everywhere in Vietnam. In any part of the country, you'd be hard-pressed to take two steps outside and not be able to spot some kind of food vendor. And it's all magnificent.

Vietnamese people are the ultimate foodies. Everyone is a critic, happy to spend hours discussing food. Authentic Vietnamese food -- as opposed to the stuff served at tourist places -- is fantastic, no matter whether you're sitting on kid-sized plastic furniture centimeters away from roaring traffic or in a fancy-pants place with air-conditioning, wine lists and snooty waiters.

International food options

Vietnamese cuisine has been influenced by its near neighbors (Thailand, China, Laos and Cambodia), by the Indians who introduced Buddhism and by its former French rulers. Foodies that they are, the Vietnamese kept the best and dismissed the rest.

Water lily stems, used in soups and salads

There are regional specialties and preferences when it comes to Vietnamese cuisine.

Northerners are said to prefer simple and less spicy food, using pepper for flavor instead of chili, while those in the south like sweeter dishes, with generous side servings of fresh herbs and salad leaves. Central Vietnamese food is the spiciest, although the heat is often turned down for foreigners.

There's also Imperial cuisine, from the former capital of Hue. Imperial cuisine usually consists of many tiny items, presented on small platters.

Vietnamese food is generally fresh and healthy with many dishes flavored with lemongrass, basil, coriander/cilantro, garlic, pepper, shallots, lime juice and fish sauce (and often a lot of chicken powder).

> TIP: MSG (*bột ngọt*) can be difficult to avoid, especially when eating street food.

MSG is sold in bulk in supermarkets

TIP: Vietnam is heaven for Celiacs and those on a gluten-free diet. Most of the noodle dishes use rice noodles, and there's no *bột* (wheat flour) in Vietnamese soy sauce.

Tropical fruits abound – rambutan, lychee, longan, durian, jackfruit, dragon fruit, pineapple, watermelon and mango. There are many wonderful fruits to explore. A range of stone fruit is also available, grown in Dalat, but I've found the Vietnamese like their fruit sour and crunchy so I never really enjoyed the beautiful-looking peaches and plums. Vietnamese people also like to dip their fruit into chili salt, another habit I never really got into.

Streetside jackfruit seller

Watermelon bike in a wet market

Vietnamese people are great snackers. Roadside stalls sell all manner of snacks and drinks.

Happy snack vendor outside a former prison on Con Dau Island

Sinh tố, or fruit smoothies, are fantastic. My favorite is soursop *sinh tố*.

Sinh tố (fruit smoothie) cart

There's also a strong coffee culture, although this is traditionally the domain of men. Sitting down and savoring an iced coffee, shooting the breeze with your buddies and having a smoke (there are so many smokers in Vietnam!) is a time-honored way for men to relax.

Coffee filters

Đi nhậu (going drinking) is another male tradition. Beer is usually poured into a glass with a huge block of ice in it. Depending on the establishment, there may be an ice boy who will fish the partly-melted ice block out of your beer and replace it with a full-size fresh block.

Drinking is a social activity. It's rare to see a Vietnamese person drinking alone. Each sip is toasted with a rowdy *"một, hai, ba, YO!"* (One, two, three – YO!). Sometimes someone may yell out "50%" or "100%" and you're expected to drink that much of whatever is in your glass. If you breach etiquette and take a sip of your beer without the communal toast, someone will usually try to cover up your *faux pas* by toasting.

TIP: Drinking is a lot of fun in Vietnam but it's easy to get completely hammered unintentionally. Foreign women can join in, although it's considered a bit odd. (Vietnamese women usually don't drink "manly" beverages like beer or coffee.) Foreign men will be expected to drink. A lot. I've heard it's quite difficult for a foreign man to leave a drinking session, which can adjourn to a club or a girly bar.

There are several traditional snacks that are usually enjoyed during a *đi nhậu* session, including duck embryo eggs (the embryo is cooked inside the shell), green mango, Vietnamese sausage, grilled corn, giant rice crackers, boiled quail eggs and various crustaceans, including sea snails. I love this tapas-style form of eating so much that it's one of the main tours we run at Saigon Street Eats. We call it the Seafood Trail.

Ốc hương (perfume snails) on the barbecue

TIP: Many street food places have "napkins" on the table, alongside condiments such as fish sauce, chili sauce and a little saucer of freshly-cut chilies. Sometimes these napkins take the form of a roll of toilet paper inside a plastic dispenser. Don't worry - any toilet paper that appears on a table has never been inside a bathroom. Just pull out a length of "napkin" and rip it off and use it as you would a regular napkin.

A wandering vendor preparing her wares

A traditional Vietnamese family meal is usually a shared meal, with each diner having a small bowl of rice in front of them. Various dishes are placed in the center of the table and everyone helps themselves by transferring food to their own bowls with chopsticks. The host usually presents favored guests (and that would be you) with tasty morsels he or she thinks they should try. (And, like most other places, mothers serve their kids what they think they should eat.)

A street food cooking station

During family meals, the youngest family member usually serves the rice. When you finish your rice, you just hand your empty bowl to the person on rice serving duty (and therefore closest to the rice dish) and they'll refill it.

TIP: For communal dining events, including work dinners, the most junior person present will serve the rice. As you're most likely to be a guest, expect someone to fill your bowl with rice at the start of the meal. During the meal your Vietnamese co-diners will probably ask you repeatedly if you'd like more rice.

Pho for breakfast

Reaching across people to get to the dishes in the center of the table is not rude. I have never gotten the hang of this, though, and I can never remember enough Vietnamese to ask someone to pass a dish. In these situations I usually ask my husband to reach and get something for me.

For the most basic family meal (and most group dining experiences reflect this to a certain extent), the shared dishes usually include a soup, a salty meat dish, a few vegetable dishes and, in the south, some fresh herbs or salad leaves. Extra dishes that could also be served may include seafood, palate-cleansing pickles or miniature eggplant/aubergine, chilies, rice paper, French fries, noodles or fried rice. Soup is usually eaten at the end of the meal, to fill up any remaining crevices in the stomach.

TIP: Sampling the soup usually indicates you're finishing up.

It's not rude to try the soup and then switch back to the meat and vegetable dishes but to your Vietnamese co-diners, ladling soup into your bowl indicates you're almost full.

Street food (with phones and some friendly same-sex touching)

In the past, especially during the deprivations of Communist rule, a family meal would consist of rice, fried eggs, salted shrimp and boiled morning glory/water spinach. The water used to boil the morning glory would be turned into a clear soup, simply by adding lime juice, monosodium glutamate (MSG is a cooking staple) and salt.

Like the Chinese, Vietnamese people believe food should be enjoyed with all five senses. Each plate should be visually appealing and have a pleasing fragrance and taste, and eating should involve feeling different textures and hearing the crunch (of cartilage or cucumber). Nothing should be wasted, either, and so you will see Vietnamese people gnawing on bones, sucking out the marrow and eating the heads of the prawns and the eyeballs of the fish. Meat is often served on the bone, sometimes with the skin on. Chicken is often served with the head and the feet on the platter. (The feet are a delicacy, just remember to pull out the toenails before you eat.)

TIP: If you are not lucky enough to be invited to

someone's home for a meal, you can get a bit of an idea of what you're missing out on by visiting a *cơm tấm* joint. Literally "broken rice," a cheaper type of rice, a *cơm tấm* place is an economical and quick way to gain access to a variety of tasty food.

Nowadays, in the south, *cơm tấm* joints are mostly for breakfast. For about US$2, a typical *cơm tấm* place will serve you a dome of rice, a fried egg, a small serving of barbecued pork, pickled carrot and daikon (white radish), and a garnish of tomato and cucumber. It's actually very tasty. You can also find all-day *cơm tấm* restaurants that have a variety of pre-cooked dishes ready to serve. The point-and-order system works well here. You start with a plate of rice and whatever you want is dumped on top. Expect to get one serving of a meat or seafood dish, a serving of vegetables, a small bowl of soup and, if you're lucky (or pay a bit extra), a piece of fruit to round off the meal.

A cơm tấm plate with barbecued pork, shredded pork skin and egg pie

Similar to a *cơm tấm* meal is the Vietnamese office lunch (*cơm trưa văn phòng*). In some cases, the food will be the same, just slightly more expensive to reflect the classier surroundings, which usually include air-conditioning.

A cơm tấm plate with sides of dipping sauce and pickled vegetables

In some restaurants (usually the cheaper ones), bones, shells, scales and other non-edible items are dropped on the floor. The staff isn't in a hurry to clean this up, as a well-rubbished floor is a sign of a popular and successful restaurant. Empty beer bottles and cans aren't cleared away until it's time to tot up the bill. Then they're counted by the staff.

> TIP: Most eating places will have a little jar of toothpicks on the table, alongside the condiments. It's considered polite to hold your hand in front of your mouth when you use a toothpick in public. (And if you're wondering why toothpicking should be hidden but nosepicking is public... well, that's just the way it is.)

Short list of must-try dishes

Bánh bèo - small steamed rice cakes topped with dried prawn and a sprinkle of green onion. A central Vietnamese dish that's usually served in the tiny ramekin it's steamed in. Best eaten by spooning on some dipping sauce and then slurping it out of its bowl.

Bánh canh chả cá - a noodle soup with slices of fish and a fish cake made from minced fish, spring onion, garlic and sometimes whole white peppers. The noodles in this dish, made with rice flour and tapioca, are a bit more substantial than other types of rice noodles.

Bánh cuốn - usually translated as "steamed rice paper rolls," *bánh cuốn* are rolls of rice paper sheets loosely wrapped around a mixture of seasoned pork and chopped mushroom. The rolls are usually chopped into bite-sized pieces, topped with fried shallots and served with *nước chấm*, the all-purpose dressing and dipping sauce containing fish sauce, lime juice, garlic and chili.

Bánh flan - called flan in South America and *crème caramel* in Australia, this dish is another tasty relic of French colonial rule. It's a tiny little custard disc topped with a chocolate, caramel or coffee sauce and crushed ice. My favorite *bánh flan* seller reckons she uses Milo but I am sure this is her polite way of telling me the recipe for her delicious bittersweet chocolate *bánh flan* sauce is top-secret.

Bánh flan

Bánh mì – baguettes. Fluffy airy rolls with a golden brown crunchy crust, packed with pickled vegetables, pate, soy sauce, coriander, chili, cured meats, and a dusting of pepper and salt. The French never did baguettes this good! If you're not a chili fiend, *"không ớt"* (no chili) is a very handy phrase to know when a *bánh mì* is being prepared.

There are three main types of *bánh mì*: *bánh mì thịt*, containing cold cuts and pate; *bánh mì heo quay*, containing roast pork; and *bánh mì ốp la*, containing a fried egg and soy sauce.

Bánh xèo - a stuffed pancake or crepe named for the sizzling sound made when it cooks (*xèo*). In southern Vietnam, *bánh xèo* are crispy and bright yellow, quite large and filled with sliced pork, prawns, bean sprouts and mung beans. In central Vietnam, they're smaller, softer and made without turmeric, so they're not as yellow. The actual *bánh xèo* can be quite blah. The key to this dish is the herbs that come with it. You need to tear off a small chunk of pancake and roll it up in a mustard or lettuce leaf with a selection of herbs. Then dip your *bánh xèo* roll in the dipping sauce provided.

Bánh xeo, wrapped and rolled and ready to go

Bò kho – beef stew, the local version of the French dish *bœuf bourguignon,* also known as beef burgundy. Cooked with chunks of carrot, onion, and thick rice noodles. Even better when served with a baguette to soak up every last drop of the tasty broth.

Bò lúc lắc - shaking beef (so called for the way the beef dances around the hot plate when it's being cooked). Cubes of seared beef served with lettuce, tomato, watercress, onion and a lime juice/ salt and pepper dipping sauce.

Bún bò Huế – beef noodle soup from the imperial capital Hue. A spicy dish that usually includes cuts of beef, pork knuckle and sometimes crab and pork balls and/or cubes of congealed blood. It's served with sprouts, coriander, sliced onion and shredded banana flower. If you're a messy eater, this dish is very stain-y. Don't wear white when planning a *bún bò Huế* attack.

Bún chả Hà Nội - A specialty from the capital featuring fresh rice noodles, a bowl of barbecued pork and pork patties in a sweet fish sauce-based broth and a basket of fresh herbs.

Bún chả Hà Nội

Bún riêu - a Southern Vietnamese noodle soup featuring ground rice, paddy crab, tofu, tomato and Vietnamese pork sausage. I prefer my *bún riêu "không huyết"* (without congealed pig's blood), which is a standard ingredient in this dish.

Bún thịt nướng - a noodle salad containing fresh *bún* rice-flour noodles with barbecued pork, pickles and shredded herbs, doused with *nước chấm*. The dish can be improved with sliced *chạo tôm* (shrimp paste on sugar cane sticks) and *chả giò* (spring rolls). In this case, the dish becomes known as *bún thịt nướng chạo tôm chả giò*.

Bún thịt nướng

Cao lầu - one of Hoi An's most famous dishes, *cao lầu* is a pork and noodle soup that is thought to be descended from the soba noodles adored by Japanese traders who used to stop in this busy port town centuries ago. The noodles have an unusual taste and texture, usually attributed to the use of ash from a certain type of local tree.

Cháo – rice porridge. Comes in fish, chicken, seafood, duck and pig organ varieties. Considered food that's easy on the stomach and so is often served to sick people and children. Cháo is very similar to the Chinese congee, but I think the Vietnamese version has the edge in terms of taste.

Chạo tôm – shrimp paste wrapped around sugar cane skewers. Usually served with an array of greenery, sprouts and rice paper for another do-it-yourself wrap-style meal.

A selection of street food sensations, including chạo tôm (prawn paste on sugar cane)

Chè - often translated as "sweet soup", *chè* is more of an anytime snack than a dessert. But what a snack it is. Similar to Singapore's chendol or the Philippines' halo halo, *chè* comes in a gazillion varieties. Some are a simple mix of fruit, syrup and ice; others are a colorful concoction of dried fruit, beans, lentils, jelly worms, bean custard, fake pomegranate seeds and/or seaweed. *Chè* is usually served in a tall glass topped with ice. Takeaway *chè* is also available, served in a little plastic bag or in a disposable plastic cup.

A wandering chè seller plies her trade in a local market

Gỏi cuốn - fresh spring rolls, also known as summer rolls. Pork, prawn, herbs and rice vermicelli wrapped in rice paper and served with a peanut and hoisin dipping sauce. Tasty and incredibly healthy.

Gỏi hoa chuối tôm thịt – banana flower salad with pork and shrimp. My uncle had a banana farm when I was a kid and I never knew you could eat the flowers. But the inventive Vietnamese at some point discovered that the pointy purple flower (that, if left, will grow into a bunch of bananas) is delicious when finely sliced and served with a tangy fish sauce and lime dressing. This salad also has pork and shrimp, as well as fried shallots and basil leaves, but the banana flower is the star.

Hủ tiếu – pork and prawn noodle soup. Tasty soup with a couple of quail eggs bobbing around, usually served with an array of greenery. I fell in love with one of the leafy greens served with this dish and then fell in love with it a little more when I discovered the English translation of the vegetable is edible chrysanthemum! Often served with offal and sometimes squid.

Hoan thanh (wonton) noodle soup

Mì hoàn thành - Vietnamese wonton noodle soup. This Chinese-influenced dish is one of my daughter's favorites. Little pork-filled wonton dumplings (and if you read *hoàn thành* phonetically you can see it does say wonton) in a clear broth with tasty soft round noodles. Often includes a piece of fried rice cracker, which goes soft and chewy in the soup.

Mì Quảng – a pork and prawn noodle dish that's part soup, part salad. Served with bean sprouts, shredded lettuce, perilla leaves, mint leaves, banana flower, roasted peanuts, lime wedges and a black sesame seed-studded rice cracker for more build-your-own-food fun. This dish is from Quang Nam province in central Vietnam and is readily available in Hoi An, where the noodles are usually white. For some strange reason, most *mì Quảng* served in Ho Chi Minh City features yellow and pinkish-purple noodles.

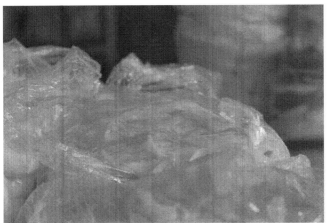

Mì Quảng noodles at the market

Nghêu hấp sả- steamed clams with lemongrass. One of my all-time favorites. You can use the clam shells as spoons to drink the lemongrass broth! (Because they're not really steamed.) Often served at the table in the tiny saucepan the clams were cooked in.

Phở – the noodle soup that's considered the unofficial national dish of Vietnam. Beef and chicken varieties are the most common but duck, pork and vegetarian options can be found too. Served with a variety of greens and sauces in the South, and with limited condiments in the north. Tearing off herb leaves and adding bits of this and that is half the fun of eating *phở*. I love to load my bowl up with as many leaves as possible, Southern-style, then add a squeeze of lime, a squirt of hoisin sauce and a few chunks of pickled garlic.

Phở ga (chicken noodle soup)

Thịt heo kho tộ - caramel pork in claypot. Melt-in-your mouth pork belly in a sweet and tangy sauce made from caramelizing fish sauce and young coconut juice. Closely related to another favorite, *thịt kho tàu,* which also contains whole duck eggs.

Rau muống xào tỏi - stir fried morning glory with garlic. Morning glory, sometimes translated as water spinach, is an insanely popular Vietnamese vegetable. I could eat *rau muống xào tỏi* at every meal. It's that good.

TIP: One of the greatest things about food in Vietnam is that most of it can be home delivered! For free! (Or a small fee.)

The major fast food chains, Lotteria (from South Korea), Jollibee (from the Philippines), and Pizza Hut and KFC (from the U.S.) all deliver. Vietnam's first McDonalds outlet opened in Ho Chi Minh City in early 2014.

Many Western and/or expat places have bought into the home delivery craze, which is great during the rainy season, although delivery can take a while. There are also several websites, such as <u>foodpanda.vn</u> and vietnammm.com, that have a centralized ordering system for a range of home delivery restaurants. All the details can be found in expat magazines. (I haven't listed them all here because these businesses seem to start up and vanish with amazing speed.)

Cooking course at Six Senses Con Dao

Coffee

It's sweet, it's thick, it's strong - and it's absolutely amazing. Vietnamese coffee is just the thing to start the day, or to keep you going. Two might make you a feel a bit shaky, but you'd still be tempted to order a third.

You have to try at least one glass of *cà phê sữa đá* - milk coffee with ice — even if you're not a coffee drinker. It's fantastic. And you're obliged to try it once you learn it's supposed to have chocolate "notes" - right?

Cà phê sữa đá (iced coffee with milk)

If you are a coffee drinker, don't settle for hotel coffee or the Americano stuff served in backpacker joints - keep walking til you find a place that will serve you the good stuff. You know you've got the real deal when a little tin pot filled with ground coffee is brought to your table. It's full of hot water which slowly drains into a cup with a bit of condensed milk in the bottom. Once all the water has filtered through the *fin* (filter), pour the hot coffee into the glass of ice you've been served. Jiggle the long spoon and the straw around until everything is cold and mixed up and Bob's your uncle.

Drinking water

Tap water is not safe to drink. Bottled water is inexpensive and available almost everywhere.

In the major centers, ice is OK, made in ice factories with filtered water. It's one of the legacies of French rule, apparently. Higher-end bars, cafes and restaurants might have their own ice machines, all with built-in water filters. The only ice you have to worry about is the hand-crushed ice served at street stalls, not because of the ice but because of the possibility that whoever crushed the ice didn't wash their hands properly.

The French influence – lots of cheese

Service standards

Wages are low in Vietnam. Waitresses and waiters only earn about VND2 million a month. That's about A$124 or US$89 a month. For this princely sum, wait staff are expected to work long shifts, six or seven days a week. They may even sleep at the restaurant – the restaurant gets free "security" and the employees don't have to pay rent.

So don't be impatient when the wait staff are all sitting around chatting, rather than hovering behind you looking out for a glass that needs refilling. If you need something, shout *"em ơi"* and you'll get someone's attention. Don't be offended when a waitress slouches over and unceremoniously dumps a plate on the table, then turns and mooches off. That's kind of the way things are done in Vietnam. It's not a personal insult.

There is no concept of entree and main dishes in Vietnam. Eating is usually communal. So all the dishes are placed in the centre of the table and every diner serves themselves. Some tourist and backpacker restaurants serve per-person meals – as in you get the whole plate of food for yourself. But not many of those places understand the Western concept of all meals being served at once so everyone can eat at the same time. At the mid to lower end of the dining scale, it's best to have a relaxed attitude towards the Western concept of waiting til everyone's served before tucking in -- encourage your dining companions to start without you if your meal doesn't arrive first.

At most local restaurants, there's only a small kitchen and one cook. Food is cooked to order, so once a dish is ready, it's delivered. This is actually good service — the food is fresh and hot and delivered immediately. So, if you're in a group, do the local thing and share your dishes. That way everyone gets to eat as soon as the first dish arrives. And, if you're still hungry after everything's been delivered, *order more.* If a dish is so good it gets finished, *order more.* That's the way the locals roll.

Wandering vendors

Much of Vietnam's commerce occurs on the streets. There are many different types of wandering vendors, many of which have a specific call or noise that identifies their wares or services.

A bag of freshly-made street salad

111

I find the noises (as noisy as they are) *and* the goods and services on offer absolutely fascinating.

Some things you may hear (although maybe not understand) are:

- ladies, men or loudspeakers calling or singing "*chưng giò gai*" or "*bánh chưng bánh giò*" to advertise the cakes they're selling from a basket on the back of their motorbike;
- a recorded message blasted from a motorbike advising anyone within hearing distance that the guy on the bike will buy old fridges, televisions and air conditioning units;
- a giant pair of scissors, often wielded by a boy on a bicycle, snipping the air to advertise noodle soup, which will be delivered to wherever you are;
- the theme music from the Titanic movie, advertising a mobile weighing machine which will print out your height, weight and fortune;
- a metallic tap-tap-tap sound advertising a mobile massage service;
- someone calling out "*ai mua chổi hay võng?*" (who wants to buy brooms or hammocks?) from a bicycle or motorbike loaded up with home-made brooms and feather dusters; and
- a (very annoying) digital tune blasted from loudspeakers attached to bicycles and motorbikes selling ice cream (*kem*).

If you eat on the street or at a place that's open to the street, expect to be approached by wandering vendors. In tourist areas, these vendors are likely to be hauling tourist tat -- cigarettes, nail clippers and/or photocopied books -- and they're approaching you because you're a tourist. In the backpacker's district in Ho Chi Minh City, these vendors can sometimes approach men and offer them drugs and/or girls.

The non-tourist options can include a mobile laminating service, steamed embryo eggs, giant rice crackers, green mango, steamed peanuts and very loud karaoke renditions of Vietnamese love songs.

Rice crackers

And then there are the lottery tickets. Most tourists spurn the wandering ticket sellers because they have no idea what is going on. Plus, the tickets sellers are often old, disabled and/or a bit grotty. But these ticket sellers are usually Vietnam's most unfortunate, who are only trying to help themselves in a country that does not have a welfare safety net.

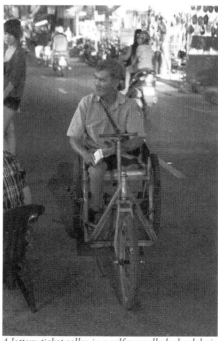
A lottery ticket seller in a self-propelled wheelchair

Each of Vietnam's 63 provincial governments run a daily lottery, offering cash prizes of up to US$70,000. Tickets are printed in batches of 10, so there are 10 of each "lucky number". The tickets cost VND10,000 each (about 45 US cents) and the ticket seller gets to keep 10% of the ticket price.

Ticket sellers usually carry tickets from a range of provinces, as well as a small book with the photocopied results of recent draws. You only need two numbers to win, although two numbers usually only get you VND100,000 (about US$4.50). You check your tickets from the end of the lucky ticket sequence, so the final two numbers on your lucky ticket have to match the two-digit winning number listed in the book.

If you win VND100,000, the ticket seller will usually give you the cash, although they will make a strong case for giving you your winnings in the form of more tickets. Bigger wins have to be collected from the lottery ticket office, and for this you'll probably need the help of a local.

> TIP: "Lucky ticket" sellers in Vietnam are usually people who can't work. They're people who lost limbs in the war, have some kind of physical disability or who are quite old. The government discourages begging and so selling tickets is really the only option these people have to support themselves or, in a multi-generational family, at least contribute to their own upkeep. Don't dismiss these ticket sellers too quickly as an annoyance. They are just trying to get by and they usually aren't too pushy with tourists because they know that foreigners don't know much about the lottery.

Checking lucky tickets

SAFETY

Vietnam is generally free of violent crime.

I worked night shift for several years and was often driving a motorbike through Ho Chi Minh City on my own after midnight. I was never bothered by anyone and I never felt unsafe.

Snatch and grabs are common. Several friends have fallen victim to snatch and grab crimes, either having a mobile phone ripped out of their hand as they walked along talking, or having a bag pulled off them as they sat on the back of a motorbike. Tourists have even had gold chains and/or necklaces ripped off their necks.

> TIP: Be vigilant. Don't walk and talk with your phone on the traffic side and keep your bag on the non-traffic side when you're walking, and in front of you if you're on the back of a motorbike. Always have the strap of your camera around your neck or wrist, especially when taking photos of the crazy traffic. Don't make it a habit to keep all your important stuff in the bag you carry every day. Often the snatch and grab thieves are two guys on a hotted-up (and therefore louder than usual) motorbike, who spot their victim, drive up on the footpath and cut the strap of your bag and then roar off, all in a matter of seconds. Keep an ear out for noisy

115

motorbikes and, if possible, wear a bag with a thick strap or a backpack that has two straps and is therefore more difficult to remove.

Bar scams also occur from time to time. Pretty girls, a few drinks, gambling... the details are always hazy in recollection. If you think you're being scammed, keep your wits about you and try to get out of there as quickly and diplomatically as possible.

I've never been robbed or pickpocketed in Vietnam -- and most visitors aren't either. I have always made a conscious effort not to look wealthy. I don't wear jewelry and I don't carry a handbag. I have a small purse that fits in one pocket and my phone goes in the other. I also don't stand on busy street corners taking photographs or filming street scenes from the back of motorbikes -- activities that appear to be super-seductive to robbers.

I sometimes see women carrying around large purses from home, full of credit cards, ATM cards and photos. The look on Vietnamese people's faces when these monstrosities are produced is priceless – *wah, such a big purse, must have a lot of money!* (And you know, if you have money, you have to pay more.)

> TIP: There is a high crime "season" just before *Tết*, when breaking and entering and snatch and grab crimes become more common. The criminals are often people who feel enormous societal pressure to impress their family and friends with their big city success (i.e., money) when they return to their hometowns for *Tết*.

There are a number of police-like authorities and it can be confusing to try to work out which type of police you need to contact if something goes wrong.

Generally, if you want to report a robbery or a stolen item, you need to contact the local ward police, who wear green uniforms. One couple I know told me their local ward police wouldn't record the theft of their mobile phone unless they came back with a Vietnamese-speaker. This just shows you can't expect the police in Vietnam to be as helpful as the police back home.

In an emergency, call 115 for an ambulance, 113 for police and 114 for the fire brigade.

> TIP: Especially in an emergency, remember to add the area code of your location if you are using a cell phone. The emergency police number in Hanoi would be 024-113 and if calling in Ho Chi Minh City the number would be 028-113.

HEALTH

There is nothing worse than getting sick when you're traveling. Luckily, help is at hand no matter where you are in Vietnam.

There are English speaking clinics in the major tourist centers (a list of medical clinics can be found on page 183) and just about every street corner has a pharmacy (*nhà thuốc*) that can dispense prescription medication and over-the-counter remedies.

Unless you're after opiates or sleeping pills, you don't need a prescription to buy prescription medicines in Vietnam. Just take the packet of your old medicine to a *nhà thuốc* so the pharmacist can match it up. If you don't have the packet, you can write down the name of it. They may suggest a local product or a generic brand. Make sure you check the expiry date and the country of manufacture. Many Vietnamese people won't buy medicines made in Vietnam or China because they don't have much confidence in local quality control standards.

You can get a prescription at one of the Western-style clinics, which will usually have its own pharmacy.

> TIP: It's often much cheaper to take the prescription to a local pharmacy rather than use the in-house dispensary at the English-speaking clinics.

Over-the-counter medicine is also available at pharmacies. Items such as rehydration salts, cold medicine, cough syrup and adult and children's Panadol/Tylenol are readily available and are usually much cheaper than at home. Pseudoephedrine and ephedrine are banned in Vietnam, so you can't get all the cold and flu medications that you're used to at home, such as the Australian Sudafed.

There are an increasing number of health food shops popping up in Ho Chi Minh City and Hanoi. These places stock diet supplements, vitamins, fat-burning powders and protein powders.

Optometrist shops are also fairly common. Look for the words *kính thuốc* (medicine glasses) or *tiệm kính* (spectacle shop). As well as eye-testing equipment, these shops usually have machines that can analyze the prescription of an existing pair of glasses. You can get prescription and non-prescription eye glasses and sunglasses (*kính mát*) at these places, as well as contacts and contact solution.

TIP: Tampons used to be hard to find in Vietnam and I used to stock up during trips home. They are much more widely available these days. I've mainly seen the Helen Harper and Kotex brands sold. Sanitary napkins (which are much cheaper in Vietnam than at home) and tampons are sold in supermarkets, not pharmacies.

TRAVELING WITH KIDS

Vietnamese people LOVE kids. This can make your little ones feel like tiny rock stars.

If you're traveling with very young kids, you won't really understand how much Vietnamese people love small children until you get there. Faces will light up, people will start to crowd you, clap their hands in front of the baby's face, pinch cheeks and thighs and pat heads. It can be overwhelming ... and it can drive the whole family completely bonkers. Try to accept the love in the vein in which it's intended -- with complete goodwill.

118

When our daughter was only a few months old, I was concerned about how waitresses would take her away from me and carry her through the restaurant like she was some kind of holy relic. But, after being repeatedly reassured that no one planned to steal the baby, I learned to enjoy having a bit of time to eat with no one on my lap, using both hands.

> TIP: There is a slightly disturbing aspect to this love of children. Some Vietnamese people like to grab the penises of little boys. It's supposedly non-sexual, done because the child is innocent (and little penises are SO CUTE) and therefore there is no sexual connotation. From a Western perspective, this is shocking and completely unacceptable. From a Vietnamese point-of-view, it's completely normal, just a bit of fun and nothing to worry about. It seems to be most common in central Vietnam. It's best to be prepared for such an event, with the child and the parent ready to say a firm "no" to whoever does the grabbing.

There are many sights and activities in Vietnam capable of amusing children. There's everything from tranquil pagodas, pristine white beaches, water parks, museums, cinemas and game arcades to indoor play centers. There are also food-related attractions, such as desserts-as-snacks, French fries served with butter and sugar and an amazing array of juices, smoothies and fizzy drinks.

Diapers/nappies

While many locals raise babies without ever using a nappy/diaper, packets of disposable nappies are available in supermarkets. Be aware, though, that the quality is a lot lower than what you're used to. Also, make sure you check the illustration on the packaging that shows whether it's a pull-up, tape fastening or an insert that's stuck inside the baby's pants like a sanitary napkin. There are usually baby wipes and other baby paraphernalia in the same aisle as the nappies/diapers in supermarkets and 7-11-type convenience stores.

TIP: Mamy Poko and Goo.n, both Japanese brands, are of higher quality than other brands, even the local version of Huggies. If you're traveling with a baby, you don't need to bring an enormous supply of disposable nappies with you, you can buy as you go.

Trains and buses

For smaller kids, the train is a far better long distance travel option than the bus. There is much more room to roam -- and it's much safer to walk (or run or wrestle) in a train aisle than a bus aisle. Even the seated carriages are more kid-friendly than the bus.

TIP: On the trains, children under four are free, although they won't get their own seat or bed. Children aged five to nine travel at half price and kids over 10 pay the full fare. In most cases on the buses, children aged from four to 10 pay 50% of the adult fare.

SHOPPING

Like most other countries, Vietnam does a roaring trade in tourist tat, selling everything from t-shirts to trinkets. You'll see the same kind of stuff for sale in tourist centers throughout the country.

A lot of the tourist stuff is quite cheap, designed to appeal to backpackers' budgets. There are also higher-end souvenirs, such as furniture, antiques, lacquerware and silk embroidery "paintings".

If you are a keen shopper, you'll find many interesting little shops to poke around in, including fair trade shops. Just make sure you know the **customs regulations** that apply to the countries you'll be visiting next, including your home country. Be especially careful of any products made of wood, bamboo or other natural materials. Even the iconic Vietnamese *nón lá* conical hat, which is made from palm leaves, may not meet some countries' customs and quarantine rules.

TIP: When going crazy in the tourist shops, also bear in mind that a lot of cheap stuff doesn't last very long. Keep your expectations low to avoid disappointment.

The most popular souvenirs from Vietnam (apart from the tourist tat) are silk products, lacquerware, embroidery, lanterns, handicrafts and tailored clothes (especially from the central town of Hoi An). Vietnam also produces high quality ceramics and marble carvings.

TIP: Standing outside a shop or stall, while looking at the stock, talking about it and taking photos *and not buying anything* is thought to generate bad luck for the vendors. To banish this bad luck, the stallholders have to go to the market and buy some lucky papers to burn. Try not to create bad luck in this manner, especially for small stallholders outside of the main tourist centers.

At tourists markets and many tourist shops, prices are negotiable. There's a bit of theater involved in haggling in Vietnam, so if you've fallen in love with something and feel you MUST have it, put your best poker face on. If you're with someone else, you can use a (prearranged) good cop-bad cop routine, with the naysayer's role to find fault with everything to try to drive the price down.

Handwoven silk, Elephant Falls (near Dalat)

There is a dual pricing system in Vietnam -- most vendors regard foreigners as rich enough to pay more for things than local do, so they are charged more.

> TIP: Don't get angry about the dual-pricing system, there is a certain logic to it. After all, your flight to Vietnam probably cost more than the country's average per capita income of US$1,100 *a year*. You really can afford to pay a little more than a local.

Keep negotiating until you're happy with the price. If you can't reach a price you're happy with, walk away. Whatever you do, don't get angry during or after price negotiations. It's a loss of face from the Vietnamese point of view and a waste of energy from mine.

> TIP: Prices are fixed in supermarkets, department stores and most non-tourist shops.

I usually take home a lot of Vietnamese **food souvenirs**, such as tea, coffee, condiments, candy and snacks. The beauty of these gifts is that they are available in the supermarket at local prices with no haggling required. You can find a lot of the same products in fancy packaging for 10 times the price, especially at the international airports.

If you're a foodie, keep your eyes peeled for food souvenirs such as green chili sauce, toffee-coated sesame rice crackers, cashews, coconut candy, squid and beef jerky, and tea and coffee. The best supermarket brands of coffee are Trung Nguyen and Highlands Coffee, and the Vietnamese coffee filters are also available in the supermarket, in the homewards aisle, for about VND15,000. A few packets of Vietnamese coffee and a filter is a great gift for coffee connoisseurs back home (and they don't have to know how cheap it is).

Supermarkets in Vietnam look similar to those at home

Vietnam is a big manufacturer of clothing and footwear, although most of the "big size" stuff is export-only. If you are small enough to fit into Vietnamese clothes and shoes, you'll be in shopping heaven .... hopefully. Some of my petite female friends have told me that although they can fit into Vietnamese clothes, the armholes are often too small and there's not enough bum-room in the clothes. Some of my slighter male friends have told me that Vietnamese pants are cut very tight in the tackle department.

> TIP: When trying clothes on, make sure they are a comfortable fit when standing, sitting, touching your toes and waving your arms around. Ladies should pay particular attention to the armholes in shirts as well as the seat of pants. Men need to check the overall length of shirts, as well as sleeve length. I'm guessing men won't actually need to be told not to buy trousers that are uncomfortably tight in the crotch.

Modeling high fashion at a Ho Chi Minh City pagoda

THINGS TO DO

Every major town has its tourist attractions, ranging from palaces and museums to historical sites. These can usually be "done" within a few days.

In Ho Chi Minh City, the main tourist draw cards are the General Post Office, the Notre Dame Cathedral, the People's Committee Building (the former Hotel Deville), the shagadelic Reunification Palace, the War Remnants and the Opera House.

In Hanoi, the list includes the Ho Chi Minh Mausoleum, Ho Chi Minh's House, One Pillar Pagoda (*Chùa Một Cột*), Ho Chi Minh Museum, the Temple of Literature, Hoan Kiem Lake and the 36 streets of the Old Quarter.

All the mainstream guidebooks and travel sites list Vietnam's tourist attractions, so I'm not repeating them here. Instead, here's a list of everyday places that will keep you (and the kids) entertained.

Ho Chi Minh City

Kids Club Saigon
(Kids activities, birthday parties, summer programs, indoor and outdoor play areas)
79/7 Pham Thai Buong, Phu My Hung, District 7
Tel: (+84-28) 5412-5944
www.kidsclubsaigon.com

Snap Café
(Café with covered kids playground and craft shop that runs regular activities during school holidays)
32 Tran Ngoc Dien, Thao Dien, District 2
Tel: (+84-28) 35194282
facebook.com/TheSnapCafe

Gymboree Play & Music
First floor, Somerset Chancellor Court, 21-23 Nguyen Thi Minh Khai, District 1
Tel: (+84-28) 3827 7008
www.gymboreeclasses.com

Diamond Plaza
(Game arcade and bowling alley on the top floor)
34 Le Duan St, District 1

Questzone
(Indoor playground, can be hired for parties)
Ho Chi Minh International Exhibition Center
446 Hoang Van Thu, Tan Binh District
Tel: (+84-28) 845 0331

Vinpearl Games World
(Games arcade)
B2 floor, Vincom Center, 70/72 Le Thanh Ton, District 1

Joymax
(Play center)
219 Nguyen Van Huong St, District 2
Tel: (+84-28) 3744 6135

K&K Playground
(Indoor and outdoor play centre)
15 Tong Huu Dinh Street, District 2
Tel: (+84-28) 6281 8739
kkplayground.com

Lan Anh Country Club
(Swimming pool, tennis courts, tennis coaching, squash, gym)
291 Cach Mang Thang Tam, District 10
Tel: (+84-28) 3823 8028

Lego Play and Edu
(Toy store and entertainment center)
Sky Garden 2, Phu My Hung, District 7

Lego Brain
(Toy store and entertainment center)
Grandview D, Phu My Hung, District 7

Kids Yard
Fourth floor, Thien Son Plaza, 800 Nguyen Van Linh Parkway,
District 7

Kizciti
(A vast activity center where kids aged 3 to 15 can "work" at various
careers, including in a fire station, hospital and an airport. All in
Vietnamese, with most assistants able to help with basic
translations.)
Hoang Dieu St, Khanh Hoi Park, District 4
Tel: (+84-28) 3825 3868
kizciti.vn/hcm/

Tini World
(Entertainment center)

4th floor, 235 Nguyen Van Cu St, District 1
Tel: (+84-28) 3600 2103
tiniworld.com

Golden Dragon Water Puppets
55B Nguyen Thi Minh Khai
Labor Cultural House, District 1
Tel: (+84-28) 3827 2653
www.goldendragonwaterpuppet.com

Vietnam Cookery Center
4th floor, 26 Ly Tu Trong St, District 1
Tel: (+84-28) 3827 0349
www.vietnamese-cooking-class-saigon.com

DanCenter
46/2 Nguyen Cuu Van, Binh Thanh District
Tel: (+84-28) 3840 6974
www.dancentervn.com

Paintball Saigon
14-16-18 Road 11, An Phu, District 2
www. paintball.asia

Push Rock Climbing
S67-1 Sky Garden 3, Phu My Hung, D.7

Saigon Outcast
(Part skate-park, part bar, part graffiti gallery, part outdoor cinema.
Check the website for upcoming events.)
188/1 Nguyen Van Huong, District 2
http://www.saigonoutcast.com

Saigon Skatepark
(Small indoor skate and BMX park)
1017 Binh Quoi Street, Binh Thanh District

Parks (Ho Chi Minh City)
Tao Dan Park

Bounded by Truong Dinh, Nguyen Thi Minh Khai and Nguyen Du Streets, District 1

A vast green oasis in the city that used by locals from everything to morning exercises and dance classes to scout camps and cheerleader practice. There's a free outdoor playground and an air-conditioned indoor play center for younger kids, as well as a fascinating "bird cafe" near the Cach Mang Thang Tam Street edge of the park. The sculptures and mini-Cham Tower are also popular backdrops for local photographers, amateur and professional.

Van Thanh Park
48/10 Dien Bien Phu Street, Binh Thanh District
Lovely quiet green oasis close to the center of Ho Chi Minh City. Park, play area, swimming pool and restaurants. Free entry to the main area, small fee for the swimming pool.
Tel: (+84-28) 3899 4760

Dam Sen Cultural Park
3 Hoa Binh District 11
The highlight is the water park but there are also rides for children, water puppets, paddle boats, fishing and a few restaurants. Small entry fee.
Tel: (+84-28) 3855 4963

Suoi Tien Amusement Park
Hanoi Highway, Tan Phu, District 9 (You can't miss the giant elephant tusks that mark the entrance.)
A whacky theme park with a Buddhist theme. It has a water park section (avoid on weekends and public holidays) and a few caged animals as well as rides, paintball, go-karts and an ATV section.
www.suoitien.com

Binh Quoi Tourist Villages
1147 Xo Viet Nghe Tinh, Binh Thanh District
Tel: (+84-28) 3556 5891
Restaurant, villas for rent, tennis court, tourist boats. Free entry.

Saigon Zoo and Botanical Garden

2 Nguyen Binh Khiem District 1
Tel: (+84-28) 3829 1425
Lovely grounds beside the zoo area. Some of the animals look a little
sad. There's also a temple and a museum within the garden area.
Small entry fee.
www.saigonzoo.net

September 23 Park
Pham Ngu Lao Street, District 1
Large, long and skinny park near Ho Chi Minh City's backpacker
area that includes a newish outdoor play area. The park was built
along the French railway that was ripped up after colonial rule
ended, hence the strange shape of the park.

Hanoi

Temple of Literature
54 B Quoc Tu Giam, Dong Da

Hanoi Cooking Centre
40 Chau Long Ba Dinh
Tel: (+84-24) 3715 0088
www.hanoicookingcentre.com

Hanoi Starbowl
2B Pham Ngoc Thach Dong Da
Tel: (+84-24) 3574 1614
www.hanoistarbowl.com

Bach Thau Roller Skating
1B Hoang Hoa Tham Ba Dinh
Tel: (+84-24) 3843 9703

Kizciti
(A vast activity centre where kids aged 3 to 15 can "work" at various
activity stations, including a fire station and a bakery. All in

Vietnamese, with assistants sometimes available able to help with basic translations.)
Vincom Mega Mall (Royal City)
72A Nguyen Trai, Thanh Xuan District
Tel: (+84-24) 6262 0031
http://kizciti.vn/hn

Vietnam Museum of Ethnology
Nguyen Van Huyen Road, Cau Giay Street
Tel: (+84-24) 37562193
www.vme.org.vn

TIP: Set aside a whole day for the Museum of Ethnology, especially if you're traveling with kids. The museum, about seven kilometers from downtown Hanoi, has full-size replicas of the traditional houses of various ethnic minority groups, which simply must be explored and clambered about by anyone still in touch with their inner child ... as well as actual children. There's a cute little training restaurant on the grounds, which is perfect for a refueling stop.

A traditional Rong House. These are used/built by the Bahnar and Jarai ethnic minority groups who live in the Central Highlands of Vietnam.

The Municipal Water Puppet Theatre
57B Dinh Tien Hoang St
Tel: (+84-24) 3 8249494
www.thanglongwaterpuppet.org

Vincom Towers
(Video game arcade and movie theatre)
191 Ba Trieu Street
http://www.vincomcitytowers.com.vn/

Flower Market
Au Co Street

Ho Tay Water Park (also known as Westlake Water Park)
(Water slides, wave pool, diving pool, suspension bridge, swinging ropes)
614 Pho Lac Long Can, Ho Tay District
Tel: (+84-24) 37 184 222 / 37 184 193
http://congvienhotay.vn/?lang=_eng

Sun Park (next to Ho Tay Water Park)
(Amusement park with roller coasters, ferris wheels, bumper cars and bumper boats.)
Hanoi Zoo
Off Kim Ma, opposite Daewoo Hotel
Tel: 3834 7395

Parks

Hoan Kiem lake (in the city center, free entry)
Pho Le Thai To

Ho Tay (free entry)
Tay Ho District

Lenin Park (free entry)
Le Duan Street

Free Things to Do

Go for an early morning walk to your local park or beach. There will be hordes of people exercising – aerobics, tai chi, kicking a feathered sack around, playing badminton or just walking around.

Visit a temple or pagoda. Most temples are open to the public (the ones that are not public will have a security guard to let you know you're not welcome). You are free to wander in and have a look around. Taking photos is usually OK -- again, someone will tell you if they're not. Just make sure you dress appropriately. Knees and shoulders should be covered. The main difference between a temple and a pagoda is that monks live at pagodas, with the residential and dining areas usually off-limits for visitors.

In Ho Chi Minh City, the Youth Cultural House (Nhà Văn Hóa Thanh Niên Thành Phố) has free English club meetings on Sundays. Sundays 8am to 11am (no air-conditioning) and 2.30pm to 4.30pm (inside, with air-conditioning). Free for foreigners; small fee per session for Vietnamese. www.nvhtn.org.vn (in Vietnamese.) 4 Pham Ngoc Thach, District 1

Canoodling in the park. Because Vietnam is crowded and most young people live with their parents (even after they've married), there isn't much privacy. Courting couples often go to a park in the evening for a bit of kissing and cuddling that would be entirely inappropriate in front of their families. At night, different parks have different reputations - some are friend hangouts and some are for couples. You'll know within a few minutes which type of park you're in.

Attend a free concert on the steps of the Ho Chi Minh City Opera House on Sunday mornings. It's usually standing room only ... unless you've brought your own motorbike to lounge on.

The Ho Chi Minh Museum in Hanoi (9 Ngoc Ha, Ba Dinh, Hanoi) is open from 8am to 5pm on weekdays and Saturdays from 8am to 12pm. Entry to this museum, dedicated to the life and times of the guy affectionately known as Uncle Ho, is free.

Entry is also free to the Temple of Literature in Hanoi (Quoc Tu Giam Street), Vietnam's oldest university.

BONUS TIPS FROM A LOCAL - What to do in Ho Chi Minh City

Since moving to Vietnam, I have entertained many visitors ... and this task has gotten easier over the years as I've learned more about my adopted home.

We usually don't accompany our visitors when they do the basic sights. There's only so many times you can see some things. But we do encourage everyone to see and/or visit the city's highlights.

We usually dispatch our visitors into District 1 with a map, a guidebook and instructions for them to do a walking tour that takes them to the Reunification Palace, then past the General Post Office, the Opera House and the Hôtel de Ville, aka City Hall.

We tell our visitors to steer clear of the Ben Thanh Market with its hideously pushy vendors and sub-standard food stalls, and also any lurking *xích lô* (cyclo) drivers, who always overcharge.

A xích lô (cyclo) waiting for a passenger

Our visitors decide for themselves whether or not to visit the War Remnants Museum. It can be a bit depressing ... and there is so much more to Vietnam than the last war, so in my opinion, missing this attraction isn't a big deal at all.

The other popular war-related attraction is the Cu Chi Tunnels, the vast network of underground tunnels and living quarters used by the Viet Cong during the war, which can be done as a half-day excursion. We recommend a tour company called Saigon River Express, which whisks you down to the tunnels on the river. It's pricier than the standard backpacker tour to the same site, but I think it's worth the money.

For visitors who want to see the Mekong Delta, we recommend they check out Saigon River Express's one-day tour or look at the homestay options offered by Innoviet.

All our visitors are taken on one or two of our street food tours, because they're based on what we wanted to show our friends and family when they came to visit. A visit to Vietnam should include lots and lots of fabulous food, especially street food, and we still get ridiculously excited when sharing our favorite eating places.

I've drawn up the following itineraries for various friends and family members.

With my vegetarian sister, we'd:

- eat at Hum vegetarian restaurant for pan-Asian cuisine in stylish decor;
- have half a half-day of pampering at Cat Moc Spa, owned and operated by the lovely Ms. Khanh who went to university with Vu;
- eat at Hoa Dang vegetarian restaurant for Vietnamese-style vegan food, including a range of mock meats, in an upscale cafeteria atmosphere;
- act like 1920s colonial overlords at Temple Club;
- do a Saigon Unseen tour; and
- eat chè at Tan Dinh Market and then browse the fabric shops along Hai Ba Trung Street.

If my vegetarian sister's three boys were coming as well, we'd:

- visit <u>Dam Sen Water Park</u> (not on a Tuesday, though, because it's closed then);
- visit the water and amusement park sections of the ultra-whacky <u>Suoi Tien Theme Park;</u>
- get our inner-Rambo on (in a non-lethal way) at <u>Paintball Saigon;</u>
- <u>take the Urban Tales murder mystery tour of Cholon, Ho Chi Minh City's Chinatown;</u>
- discuss whether teenage boys are too mature for a <u>water puppet show;</u> and
- see if teenage boys (accompanied by their of-age but still amazingly young mum and aunt) could get into <u>Acoustic</u> to see some live cover bands … because the middle boy is a drummer and needs to see the best of the best..

With my hipster DJ sister, we'd:

- visit <u>Pasteur Street Brewing Company</u> for some American-style craft beer infused with local flavors such as jasmine, Phu Quoc pepper and jackfruit;
- get our hair and nails done at <u>Jasmine Spa</u> then pop next door for a squiz at Saigon Kitsch, a cute little gift and souvenir shop;
- take a long leisurely lunch at the <u>Secret Garden</u> rooftop restaurant;
- make inappropriate jokes at <u>Fanny Ice Cream</u> (especially if eating durian ice cream);
- get sweaty with David of <u>Golden Hands Pilates</u> (from a distance, of course);
- splash out on cocktails and sushi at the fancy new <u>Sorae Sushi</u>; and
- discuss the benefits of brunch at the Intercontinental Asiana, which starts at midday and includes a chocolate fountain, free-flow Veuve, tequila shots and an oyster and vodka bar.

With my mum, we'd:

- eat fancy French fare (for a fraction of what we'd pay in Australia) at Le Bouchon, which serves the best French onion soup in the world;
- take Sophie's Art Tour, fascinating for its overview of Vietnam's recent history as well as for the art;
- spend a lot of time at Snap Cafe, known at our place as "the cafe playground", the most child-friendly venue in all of Ho Chi Minh City (because it has free wifi, a free two-for-one book exchange, a fully-stocked bar, great food AND it allows adults to sit while kids run, jump, climb and throw sand at each other);
- look for hidden treasures in Saigon's "antique street" (Le Cong Kieu) near the banned-by-me Ben Thanh Market;
- watch clumps of water hyacinth float down the Saigon River while sipping cocktails at The Deck in District 2;
- have a family portrait session at Saigon Crazee;
- spend a day at KizCiti in District 4 because watching kids dress up and pretend to be firefighters, traffic cops, pilots and baby doctors is just so adorable (and the kids have so much fun);
- insert ourselves into 3D "optical illusion art" at Artinus in District 7; and
- take a cooking course at Vietnam Cookery Center.

With my lovely French photographer friend, we'd:

- lounge by the pool at Thao Dien Village, a pricey not-everyday option. The pool is right by the Saigon River and surrounded by palm trees and deck chairs, so it feels like you're on a tropical island;
- spend some quality evening hours watching him try to schmooze the ladies at Lush, Carmen and Blanchy's Tash (and steer him away from Apocalypse Now, because Darling Man says that's where the old prostitutes hang out);

- book in for therapeutic massages with Hieu from Golden Hands Massage;
- dine at the super-groovy Cafe If, which serves contemporary Vietnamese dishes;
- do cheesy Vietnam-style photo-shoots at Van Thanh Park (48/10 Dien Bien Phu Street, Binh Thanh District) and Binh Quoi Tourist Village (1147 Binh Quoi Street, Binh Thanh District); and
- spend three days in Vung Tau eating seafood and bánh khọt, visiting giant Jesus and Buddha statues and driving motorbikes out to visit waterfalls that Darling Man has heard of but never seen.

Street food seafood: barbecued crab claws

There you go… 100 unusual travel tips to Vietnam – and how to move there. (It's actually more than 100 tips, as some super-nerdy/OCD readers might have noticed. We were having so much fun we just kept going after we hit 100.)

And what about the rest of the title of this book? You may fall in love with Vietnam, as I did. **Here's how to move there…**

Living in Vietnam is very different from experiencing the country as a visitor. You have to handle driving licenses, bills, meter readers, supermarket queues and sometimes a daily commute and school run.

MOVING TO VIETNAM

People move to Vietnam to live for many different reasons. Some, like me, are mesmerized by the country and want more time to experience its quirky charm. Some are transferred to the country by multinationals, others are seeking a step up the corporate ladder or an escape from everyday life back home.

The multitude of reasons that entice non-Vietnamese people to Vietnam means that expats arrive with varying degrees of anticipation, fear, excitement and expectations. The main thing that potential expats should keep in mind is that Vietnam is not like any other place on earth - not China, not Indonesia, not Thailand…and certainly not like home. For some people this can be exhilarating, for others it can be sheer torture. My advice is to try to make the most of your time in Vietnam. **Treat it like an adventure**, because that's exactly what life here is.

Don't be afraid to seek help. If you will be working in Vietnam, assistance should be available from your employer. If there's no human resources or admin assistant to help, ask your colleagues for advice and assistance. Vietnamese people are usually incredibly helpful and will bend over backwards to help out someone who's a bit stuck.

If you're going to arrive in Vietnam without a job, there are still lots of places to seek help, from online forums to travel agents and friendly cafe and hotel staff.

Hanoi and Ho Chi Minh City both have thriving expat communities. There is a plethora of sporting and social clubs, magazines, supermarkets, cafes, bars and restaurants set up to cater to the ever-growing number of foreigners in these two cities.

In Ho Chi Minh City, large expat enclaves exist in An Phu in District 2 and Phu My Hung in District 7. However, expats are scattered throughout this bustling metropolis, in all kinds of accommodation from guest houses to high-rise apartments and high-end villas, as well as amongst the locals, in thin multistoried Vietnamese houses in narrow *héms* (alleys).

In Hanoi, expats live in many different parts of the city, with Tay Ho and West Lake the most popular areas.

Here's a quick guide to some of the practicalities of day-to-day living in Vietnam.

Banking

Banking rules are a potential headache for foreigners living in Vietnam. To deposit money into a bank account, you need a pay slip showing you earned the money legally in Vietnam (and paid tax). To transfer money out of Vietnam, you need pay slips to show you earned the money legally in Vietnam. Some banks also ask to see your work permit.

ATMs are everywhere in Vietnam, except in the most remote towns and villages. There is a plethora of local banks that have ATMs that can be used to make an international withdrawal. There are also ATMs belonging to international banking entities such as Citibank, HSBC and Australia's ANZ and Commonwealth banks.

Credit cards can be used in Vietnam, usually at the higher-end hotels, restaurants and shops. Some establishments will charge 3% to 5% for a credit card transaction.

Some expats in Vietnam have offshore bank accounts and regard ATM withdrawal fees as just one of the costs of living in the wild wild east.

Internet accessibility

Getting internet access installed in your home is relatively easy. The main internet providers are FPT (www.fpt.vn), VNPT (www.vnpt.vn) and Viettel (www.viettel.com.vn). (Be aware that Viettel is owned by the military.)

We pay about VND200,000 a month for high-speed internet access from VNPT. The service is generally reliable, although from time to time the Internet speed becomes agonizingly slow. Usually after a couple of hours, whatever the issue was is resolved and the normal Internet speed returns. As you would expect, this inexplicable slowdown usually occurs when I am trying to meet an important work deadline.

Taxes

If you are working in Vietnam, your employer should take the tax out of your salary. I've heard of cases where the tax is taken out of the salary and not paid to the government but that's the company's problem, not yours.

When discussing and negotiating salaries, always check that you're negotiating your net (after-tax) salary.

Tax rates

Foreigners who work in Vietnam for a total of 183 days or more in any 12-month period must pay personal income tax, or PIT. The following rates will apply to your monthly salary; however, your employer should pay the following tax rates on your behalf:

VND0–VND5,000,000 - 5%
VND5,000,000–VND10,000,000 - 10%
VND10,000,000–VND18,000,000/month - 15% tax
VND18,000,000–VND32,000,000 - 20% tax
VND32,000,000–VND52,000,000 - 25% tax
VND52,000,000–VND80,000,000 - 30% tax
More than VND80,000,000 - 35% tax

(from PWC's Vietnam Pocket Tax Book 2014)

Visas

There are two types of entry visas – tourist and business. If you have organized employment before arriving in Vietnam, your employer should be able to help you obtain a business visa. The application process is the same as for a tourist visa, except a letter from the employer is required.

You can apply for a business visa in Vietnam if you enter the country on a tourist visa. The advantage of a business visa is that it is usually multiple entry and valid for longer than a tourist visa. In Vietnam, most travel agents can help with visa extensions and renewals. Ask around to get the name and number of a reliable visa agent. Before I obtained my two-year residency card, I used the visa service from Chi's Café (185/30 Pham Ngu Lao, District 1, Ho Chi Minh City), where I also rented my first motorbike.

Visa rules can change without warning, so it's best to check with your nearest Vietnamese embassy before heading off. In late 2009 a sudden change of visa rules created major headaches for many long-time residents, who were unable to get the visa extensions they were expecting. Things seem to have settled since then, but one of the frustrations of living in Vietnam is that it's often hard to get information about government policies. Travel agents who had previously organized multiple-entry business visas for long-term expats without any hassles simply couldn't explain the new rules and whether they were in effect temporarily or permanently. This has happened several times since then, so be prepared.

It's usually possible to get several extensions on a one-month tourist visa to allow you to stay in Vietnam for seven months. At the seven-month mark, it's time for a visa run. Once you've left the country and entered again, you can begin the process of extending visas for another seven months. This process can be circumvented if you get a residency card, which usually accompanies a "proper" job in Vietnam. It's still possible to get a residency card without a job, but finding someone who is willing to sponsor such a card can be an adventure in itself. Just keep asking around if you really want to stay put in Vietnam for one to two years, rather than set off to explore neighboring countries every seven months.

The work visa regulations were under review for many years and few foreign nationals actually held a work visa. However, the regulation and enforcement of work visas appears to be stricter nowadays.

You can work in Vietnam without a work visa for three months. Professions like doctors and lawyers are legislated separately and people working in these fields have to meet other requirements in order to stay and work legally.

Your employer is responsible for your work visa, so if you have lined up a job before arriving, they will deal with it. If you find a job after arriving in Vietnam, it will also be up to the employer to file all the paperwork. In the past, the act of filing a work visa application appeared to appease officials.

There don't appear to be any regulations governing location independent businesses/professionals. It would seem wise to stay under the radar if you are lucky enough to have engineered this kind of business/lifestyle.

To obtain a work visa, you need a recent police check from your local police (or the police from your last country of residence) and a notarized copy of your degree. It seems a degree is now compulsory to obtain a work permit in Vietnam, although people being transferred to the country by their employer may be able to get a work permit based on their work experience.

Recruitment agencies

First Alliances
www.firstalliances.net

Navigos Group
www.navigosgroup.com

Opus Vietnam
www.opusasia.net

Smart HR
www.smarthrvietnam.com

TMF Vietnam
www.tmf-group.com

Vietnamworks
www.vietnamworks.com

JOBS FOR FOREIGNERS

Foreigners work in Vietnam in all kinds of jobs – doctors, dentists, accountants, sales executives, managers, property developers, engineers, golf pros, architects, pilots, teachers and even waiters.

There are also many freelance photographers, writers and personal trainers based in Vietnam.

Others are in Vietnam doing business – running export businesses, restaurants, bars, employment agencies, river cruises and boat building operations.

Teaching English is a popular employment option and there are several places, including Apollo English and TEFL International, where you can obtain Teaching English as a Second Language (TESOL) and the Certificate in English Language Teaching to Adults (CELTA) qualifications. The four-week courses usually include some practice teaching sessions.

Getting information about Vietnam's working and investing rules can be difficult. If you do find the right website, the English is often unintelligible – a direct translation of the Vietnamese legal code. And if you begin the maddening task of asking people in government departments for advice on your case, you may get a different answer from every person you speak to. This seems to be a form of self-protection. No one is really clear what the rules are or when the political winds could alter and change the rules completely.
Often the best leads are through word of mouth and networking. If you're looking for work and/or business opportunities, the chamber of commerce social events are where you need to be – Auscham,

Amcham, Cancham, Nordcham, etc.

Chambers of Commerce

Investors and entrepreneurs from all over the world do business in Vietnam and various chambers of commerce exist to provide networking, lobbying and information sharing opportunities. The following chambers of commerce are active in Vietnam:

Ho Chi Minh City

AmCham (American Chamber of Commerce)
New World Hotel, 76 Le Lai, District 1 Business Centre, Room 323
Tel: (+84-28) 3824 3562
www.amchamvietnam.com

AusCham (Australian Chamber of Commerce)
TV Building, Suite 1A, 31A Nguyen Dinh Chieu, District 1
Tel: (+84-28) 3911 0272 / 73 / 74
www.auschamvn.org

British Business Group of Vietnam
25 Le Duan, District 1
Tel: (+84-28) 3829 8430
execmgr@bbgv.org www.bbgv.org

CanCham (Canadian Chamber of Commerce)
New World Hotel, 76 Le Lai, District 1 Business Centre, Room 305
Tel: (+84-28) 3824 3754
www.canchamvietnam.org

Eurocham
257 Hoang Van Thu, Tan Binh
Tel: (+84-28) 3845 5528
www.eurochamvn.org

German Business Group

21-23 Nguyen Thi Minh Khai, District 1
Tel: (+84-28) 3823 9772
www.gba-vietnam.org

KoCham (Korean Chamber of Commerce and Industry)
47 Nguyen Chu Trinh District 1
Tel: (+84-28) 3837 9154
www.kochamhcm.com

Overseas Vietnamese Business Association
147 Nguyen Dinh Chieu District 3
Tel: (+84-28) 3930 1503
www.oviba.com

Singapore Business Group
Unit 1B2, 21-23 Nguyen Thi Minh Khai, District 1
Tel: (+84-28) 3823 3046
www.sbghcmc.org

Swiss Business Association
42 Giang Van Minh, An Phu, District 2
Tel: (+84-28) 3744 6996
www.swissvietnam.com

Hong Kong Business Association
New World Hotel, 76 Le Lai, D1 Business Centre, Room 322
Tel: (+84-28) 3824 3757 / 3822 8888
www.hkbav.com

NordCham (Nordic Business Association)
Bitexco Building, 19-25 Nguyen Hue, District 1
Tel: (+84-28) 3821 5423
www.nordcham.com

Thai Business Association
16/9 Ky Dong District 3
Tel: (+84-28) 931 8263

Hanoi

AmCham (American Chamber of Commerce)
Hilton Hanoi Opera, M floor 1 Le Thanh Tong Hoan Kiem,
Tel: (+84-24) 3934 2790
www.amchamhanoi.com

AusCham (Australian Chamber of Commerce)
Room 1.1.011, Handi Resco Building
521 Kim Ma Street, Ba Dinh District
Tel: (+84-24) 37245324
www.auschamvn.org

British Business Group
67 Le Van Huu Hai Ba Trung
Tel: (+84-24) 6674 8945

EuroCham (European Chamber of Commerce)
Sofitel Plaza Hotel, 1 Thanh Nien Ba Dinh
Tel: (+84-24) 3715 2228

French Chamber of Commerce and Industry in Vietnam
Sofitel Plaza Hotel, 1 Thanh Nien Ba Dinh
Tel: (+84-24) 3715 2229
www.ccifv.org

InCham (Indian Business Group)
Hanoi Heritage Hotel, 625 De La Thanh Ba Dinh
Tel: (+84-24) 3772 4248
www.inchamvietnam.org

Japanese Business Association
535 Kim Ma, 6th floor Ba Dinh
Tel: (+84-24) 3220 9907
www.jbav-hanoi.com

Taiwanese Chamber of Commerce
1 Lo, 11A Phu Do Thi Trung Yen 10 Cau Giay
Tel: (+84-24) 3783 0286

TRANSPORTATION ADVICE

If you buy a motorbike, you will pay compulsory third-party insurance that will cover personal damage of up to VND70 million and damage to another vehicle of up to VND40 million. The third-party insurance has to be renewed every year for about VND60,000. You can pay these bills at your local post office (*bưu điện*).

Cars are expensive in Vietnam. A bevy of taxes and fees push up the price of a new vehicle to two or three times what you'd pay for the same model in the U.S. or Australia.

Vietnam does not yet have a local car manufacturing industry, so all cars attract an 82% import tax, as well as 30%-50% luxury tax (depending on the number of seats). There's also a 10% value-added tax and a range of other fees for registration, the number plate, inspections, insurance, road maintenance and a stabilization fund fee.

A local newspaper calculated that a five-seater Hyundai SantaFe, which would sell for US$23,000 in the U.S., would cost US$69,000 in Vietnam. The price tag includes taxes of US$46,070. In comparison, a SYM Attila motorbike (considered a higher-end model) would cost less than US$2,000 new and as little as US$500 second-hand.

Most expats seem to find it more convenient (and possibly cheaper) to lease a car and driver. The lucky ones have a car and driver as part of their salary package. I have seen long-term car and driver packages advertised in Ho Chi Minh City for between US$490 to US$1,700/month for a seven-seater SUV. The lease package includes the car, the driver's salary, fuel, maintenance and insurance.

To find a car hire company, look for recommendations on expat forums. There are big companies, such as the Ho Chi Minh City-based Satco* that offer car hire services, as well as smaller local businesses. Many real estate agents also offer car hire services.

* This is not a recommendation. I've never used this car hire company. However, their website does have a handy price table that you could use as a guide.

Schoolgirls on Con Dao Island

WHAT TO DO WHEN YOU FIRST ARRIVE

The major cities in Vietnam have a number of short-term accommodation options, from super-budget guesthouses and hotels to swanky serviced apartments. The only limit is your budget.

At the super-budget end of the hotel/guest house spectrum, you get only the basics – a bed and a shower. Taking a shower often involves standing next to, or straddling, the toilet in a room that's no bigger than a closet.

Many people live quite happily for many years in basic guesthouses, while others require a little something more. I started off in a guesthouse in Ho Chi Minh City's backpacker district, then upgraded to a studio apartment, then a furnished house in a narrow little *hẻm* (alley), and now we live in a large furnished house in a quiet area 15 minutes from the CBD (Central Business District).

There are a few companies that offer settling-in services for new arrivals. The services on offer include help finding accommodation, home help, motorbike rentals and visa services. It's even possible to organize a bill-paying service.

Check the following websites to see what's available - but bear in mind that once you're settled, you'll probably be able to undertake most of these tasks yourself or find less expensive alternatives, such as www.residentvietnam.com.

Housing

Renting is by far the easiest housing option in Vietnam, with leases running for one to three years, with shorter-term leases usually available for serviced apartments.

A tall skinny Vietnamese house

Don't try to line up long-term accommodation until you are in

Vietnam. There have been cases where expats have been duped into paying a deposit and the first month's rent over the Internet, only to find there is no house. By all means use the Internet to search, but don't believe what you see in the pictures. You need to inspect a property – and gauge the level of noise in the neighborhood – before signing a lease.

Generally speaking, the main types of rental properties are apartments, houses and villas. Houses are usually narrow multistoried dwellings with very little land left over for a garden. Houses advertised as having a garden may only have a small courtyard that's only big enough to park a couple of motorbikes. Villas are pricier but they usually have a garden, and these properties are the domain of wealthy Vietnamese and expats on corporate packages.

Ho Chi Minh City and Hanoi have rabbit warrens of tiny alleys behind the main streets. A *hẻm* (alley) can be wide enough for a car, or so narrow you can reach out and touch the houses on either side of you. Hems are called *kiet* in Central Vietnam.

To get an idea of the pricing and style of rental properties in Vietnam, have a look at the listings on www.snap.com.vn, www.brighthomevietnam.com, www.chaocom.com and http://www.vnrenting.com/hochiminh/eng/, which all focus on Ho Chi Minh City. For Hanoi listings, check www.hanoiproperty.com, www.hanoistay.com, vietlonghousing.com and www.vinahousing.com. (Disclaimer: I've never used any of these services.)

House hunting can be time-consuming. The places advertised on the English sites may be taken. Agents will take you to completely unsuitable places, sometimes advertised for double what you've stated as your budget. (Always under quote your budget, by the way.) Or you discover that what seems a nice house is in a noisy area, or miles away from anywhere, or filled with cockroaches.

Take some time to work out what areas would be suitable and then go for a drive around, keeping your eyes peeled for *"nhà cho thuê"* signs. Often landlords will advertise with a small sign on the front of the property before going to the bother of placing a classified ad or listing with an agent.

It's worth checking Vietnamese classified websites, such as this one, to try and work out the going rates: http://muaban.net/ho-chi-minh/raovat/46/cho-thue-nha-dat/1.html. You should be able to figure out the basic details. *"Cho thuê"* means for rent, "*nhà*" means house and listings usually indicate the area of the house (e.g.: 4x16m for a four-meter wide, 16 meter deep place), the number of floors, the cost per month, and the address. Sometimes they include the number of rooms (*phòng*), meaning the number of bedrooms.

Here are some examples, taken from the website mentioned above (with phone number deleted):

> *Cho thuê nhà HXH ngay trung tâm Q1 giá 600/tháng đầy đủ tiện - XXXXXXXX nhà đầy đủ nội thất ,kết cấu 60m2,1PN,PK,bếp,tolet nhà mới 100% cho người nước ngoài thuê ở.liên hệ XXXXXXXX gặp Mr Tuấn. LH: Mr Tuấn, XX phạm viết chánh, Tel. XXXXXXXX*

Translation: House for rent in a car alley (an alley wide enough for a car), in the center of District 1, $600/month, fully furnished, *phone number*, 60 square meters, one bedroom, one living room, one kitchen, newly built, 100% for foreigners to rent. Contact *phone number* to meet Mr Tuan. Contact Mr Tuan, xx Pham Viet Chanh Street. Tel. *XXXXXXXX*.

> *Cho thuê nguyên căn nhà mặt tiền đường Trường Sơn (Cư Xá Bắc Hải) P15,Q10, DT:4,5x25m, (có sân vườn 20m2) cấu trúc: 1 trệt, 2 lầu,1 sân thượng, có 5 phòng lớn, nhà mới, đủ máy lạnh, khu vực an ninh, vị trí đẹp, giao thông thuận lợi,tiện làm văn phòng , ở, mầm non....Giá:25 triệu/tháng. LH:A Quốc: XXX.XX.XXXX*

Entire house for rent. Located in a main street of Truong Son Street (in the Bac Hai flat area) Ward 15, District 10, measurements: 4.5 meters by 25 meters, (has 20 square meter courtyard), structure: one ground floor, two higher floors, one rooftop, has five large rooms, new house, equipped with air conditioning, safe area, convenient, suitable for a business... Price VND25,000,000/month. Leasing agent: Quoc: *phone number*

Landlords are required by law to register foreign tenants with the local police. Your landlord may ask you to fill out a form for the police. He or she may also need to take your passport to the police to complete the registration process.

When house hunting, don't forget to bargain. As well as negotiating down the price, you can ask for a house to be furnished, for air conditioning to be installed or for a maid service to be included. As a non-Vietnamese, you will be at a disadvantage because if you're rich enough to be in Vietnam, you're considered rich enough to pay a little extra. Not everyone is out to rip you off, but real estate agents around the world have a bad reputation for a reason.

It's a good idea to photograph every room of your house or apartment before you move in. Print two copies and give one set to your landlord. This should limit problems when you move out. We had to pay one landlord "compensation" for the furniture that was damaged when the house flooded during a storm. It wasn't a huge amount, just enough to be annoying but not enough to argue over.

Different regions of Vietnam have different housing styles, ranging from bamboo huts in remote areas, sturdy one-level concrete houses in country areas, to the tall skinny city houses and the swanky villas and high-end apartments of the city-rich.

Most homes have a large family room, which can double up as the dining room or main sleeping room. In the cities, where property and petty crime is high, motorbikes are usually parked in the family room at night, even if the house has an outdoor parking area.

Houses usually have a solid metal security door that is kept locked whenever the front room is vacant. The security door can double as the front door or, if the house has a small courtyard/garden at the front, the security door is part of a very high fence.

The kitchen is usually on the ground floor at the back of the house, although there's typically no back door or window, so ventilation is not very good. It's rare for a Vietnamese kitchen to have hot water or an oven. There's usually a two-ring or four-ring gas cook top for cooking. Sometimes there's a bathroom between the living area and the kitchen, often under the staircase.

Higher levels will usually have one or two bedrooms per floor and a bathroom per floor. There may be a rooftop terrace. At the very least, the top of the house will have a small laundry and drying area.

Basic furniture can be pretty cheap in Vietnam but the low price can mean things won't last very long. Furnished places are available but it's best to see the furniture before agreeing to rent a furnished house or apartment. Some Vietnamese couches can be very uncomfortable for Westerners, being low to the ground and very hard. The same goes for beds - most Vietnamese prefer rock-hard mattresses so it's best to at least sit on the bed if you're looking to rent a furnished place.

Unlike houses, villas don't conform to any one style. They are usually multistoried with a garden and are surrounded by a high fence with tall gates that are kept closed and locked. Renting a villa often means a host of extra household staff is required, from security guards to gardeners and pool boys. If you're going to be paid at a rate that makes a villa possible (or if housing is included in your package), make sure you find out what staff would be required, and if a security guard is recommended, get one and factor that into your cost calculations.

International shipping of goods

When it comes to shipping goods to Vietnam, a dizzying array of import taxes are involved, as well as a range of "payments" that ease any delays in customs. If you have your heart set on shipping your worldly possessions to Vietnam, it's probably best to hire an international relocation firm and let them take care of the details. Keep in mind that personal items like photographs and artworks can be ruined by the tropical weather. Hanoi, in particular, is famous for its fungus.

While shipping all your worldly possessions to Vietnam seems like the reasonable thing to do when your employer will pick up the tab, your stuff can act as a costly anchor once it's all here if you feel the urge to cut and run or your job suddenly disappears - an occurrence that was quite common during the height of the global financial crisis.

If you decide to move to Vietnam unencumbered by stuff, it's possible to fit out a home for substantially less than you could at home. Brand name computers and cameras usually retail at similar prices as in Western countries, so don't expect a bargain, just be aware that these items are available if you need to purchase them during your stay.

Relocation agents that service Vietnam include:

Allied Pickfords
www.alliedpickfords.com

Asian Tigers Group
www.asiantigersgroup.com

Crown Relocation Services
www.crownrelo.com

Santa Fe Relocation Services
www.santaferelo.com

INSURANCE

Travel advisories always stress the need for some form of insurance when traveling. I highly recommend you are insured while living in Vietnam, because the local health services are not so great and the Western-standard medical centers are expensive. If you need complicated surgery that's not available in Vietnam, you don't want to have to pay for medivac flights to Bangkok or Hong Kong yourself.

I've been covered by either travel or expat insurance since I left Australia in 2007. I found expat insurance to be slightly cheaper. The expat insurance I had previously paid for most of my first pregnancy-related medical costs but I wasn't covered for travel, so every trip out of Vietnam required a new travel insurance policy, which wasn't costly but *was* time consuming to organize. Expat insurance usually doesn't cover property, so if you take all your worldly possessions to Vietnam, you will have to insure them separately.

I personally don't believe it's worth leaving your home country without travel insurance. If something does go wrong while overseas, the costs can be astronomical. It's much better to have insurance that you never use than having to make life and death medical decisions based on what you can and can't afford.

EDUCATIONAL OPPORTUNITIES

Historically, education has been very important to Vietnamese culture. The nation's first university was established in what is now Hanoi in 1076. The Temple of Literature in Hanoi still houses the former Imperial Academy.

Education is seen by the Vietnamese as the key to success, and middle and upper class parents try to send their children to as many extra-curricular activities as possible, with English lessons being a high priority. The ultimate objective of these extra classes is the once-a-year university exam. Pass this and you're on the road to riches, or so it's thought.

There's been some public debate in the Vietnamese media about the quality of education in Vietnam, with a number of educators pointing out the traditional focus on rote-learning doesn't equip students with the critical thinking skills they need to flourish in an international environment. The government has identified education as its number one priority and has promised to increase funding to the sector.

For Vietnamese citizens, primary school – grades one through five, ages six to 12 - is compulsory and tuition is free. Individual schools charge various fees for facilities (such as air-conditioning). Secondary school is grades six through nine, and high school is grades 10 through 12.

While I have heard of some expats sending their children to local schools, this is usually only possible if one parent is Vietnamese and the child has the correct paperwork. Most expat kids go to international schools, although some are homeschooled.

Homeschooling is unregulated in Vietnam. It seems unlikely a Vietnamese family could homeschool without some kind of repercussion – children wouldn't be eligible to sit the university entrance exam, for instance, which would leave them ineligible to study at university.

Vietnam has many international schools catering to the growing population of expats and the increasingly wealthy Vietnamese middle class. Education is big business in Vietnam and a number of foreign universities, including Australia's RMIT, have campuses in the major cities.

International schools set their own enrollment criteria, with many asking potential students to sit entrance and English proficiency tests.

International schools offer curricula from around the world, including from the US, the UK, Australia, France, Korea and Germany.

Hanoi

Kindergartens and day care centers:

Concordia International School Hanoi
Tel: (+84-24) 3795 8878
concordiahanoi.org

Hanoi International Kindergarten
Tel: (+84-24) 3719 1248
www.hik.edu.vn

International School of Vietnam
Tel: (+84-24) 3540 9183
www.isvietnam.org

KinderWorld International Kindergarten
Tel: (+84-24) 3934 7243
www.kinderworld.net

Koala House
Tel: (+84-24) 3772 3060
koalahouse.com.vn

Little Einsteins International Kindergarten
Tel: (+84-24) 3519 0457
littleeinsteins.org

Lycee Francais Alexandre Yersin
Tel: (+84-24) 3843 6779
www.lfay.com.vn

Maple Bear Canadian Kindergarten
Tel: (+84-24) 2220 6848
maplebear.vn

QSI International School Hanoi
Tel: (+84-24) 3718 6418

hanoi.qsischool.org

Starfish International Kindergarten
Tel: (+84-24) 3718 3716
www.sik.edu.vn

Schools:

Arabic School-Al Fateh
Tel : (+84-24) 3846 3468

British International School
Tel: (+84-24) 3946 0435
www.bishanoi.com

Concordia International School Hanoi
Tel: (+84-24) 3795 8878
www.concordiahanoi.org

Hanoi International School (HIS)
Tel: (84-24) 3832 7379
www.hisvietnam.com

International School of Vietnam
Tel: (84-24) 3540 9183
www.isvietnam.org

Korean International School in Hanoi
Tel: (+84-24) 3554 0224

Lycee Francais Alexandre Yersin
Tel: (+84-24) 3843 6779
www.lfay.com.vn

QSI International School Hanoi
Tel: (+84-24) 3718 6418
hanoi.qsischool.org

Russian School
Tel: (+84-24) 3833 6993

The Japanese School of Hanoi
Tel: (+84-24) 3764 9877
www.jshanoi.com

Singapore International School (SIS)
SIS has several campuses in Hanoi. For details see:
http://kinderworld.net/sis/campuses-sis/school-campuses.html

United Nationals International School of Hanoi (UNIS)
Tel: (+84-24) 3758 1551
www.unishanoi.org

Uniworld International School
Tel: (+84-24) 3843 6779
www.kinderworld.net

Universities:

RMIT University
Tel: (+84-24) 3726 1460
www.rmit.edu.vn

Ho Chi Minh City:

Kindergartens and day care centers:

The ABC International School
Tel: (+84-28) 5431 8050
www.theabcis.com

Creche Bambou-Bulles
Tel: (+84-28) 3519 1521
creche-ecole-francaises-internationales-hochiminh.com/en/home-
bambou-bulles.html

Fundino
Tel. (+84-28) 3930 0514
www.bisvietnam.com

Renaissance Future Kids
Tel: (+84-28) 3773 3171
www.renaissance.edu.vn

KinderWorld International Kindergarten
Tel: (+84-28) 5431 7477
www.kinderworld.net

Gymboree Play and Music of Vietnam
Tel: (+84-28) 3827 7008
www.gymboreeclasses.com.vn

Maple Bear Canadian Kindergarten
Tel: (+84-28) 3526 8833
maplebear.vn

Montessori Kids School
Tel: (+84-28) 3744 2639
www.montessori.edu.vn

Noah's Club
(Child care and activities for children aged six months to six years)
Tel: (+84-28) 3744 4709
noahsclubchildcare.blogspot.com

Saigon Kids
Tel: (+84-28) 3740 8081
www.saigonkidskindergarten.com

Saigon Star International School
Tel: (+84-28) 3742 7827
www.saigonstarschool.edu.vn

Smart Kids International Childcare Centre
Tel: (+84-28) 3744 6076
www.smartkidsinfo.com

Schools:

ABC International School
Tel: (+84-28) 5431 8050
www.theabcis.com

Australian International School (AIS)
Tel: (+84-28) 3742 4040 (Thu Thiem campus), (+84-28) 3744 6960
(Thao Dien campus)
www.aisvietnam.com

BIS British International School
Tel: (+84-28) 3744 2335
www.bisvietnam.com

Canadian International School (CIS)
Tel: (+84-28) 5412-3456
cis.edu.vn

Ecole Antonia
Tel: (+84-28) 3519 1521
creche-ecoles-college-francaise-europeenne.com.vn

European International School Ho Chi Minh City (formerly the
German International School Vietnam)
Tel: (+84-28) 7300 7257
www.europeaninternationalschoolhcmc.com

International German School Ho Chi Minh City
Tel: (+84-28) 3744 6344
www.igs-hcmc.de

International School Ho Chi Minh City
Tel: (+84-28) 3898 9100
www.ishcmc.com

International School Saigon Pearl
Tel: (+84-28) 2222 7788
issp.edu.vn

Japanese International School
Tel: (+84-28) 3417 9013
www.j-schoolhcm.net

Lycee Francais International Marguerite Duras
Tel: (+84-28) 3725 2208
lfiduras.com

Renaissance International School Saigon
Tel: (+84-28) 3773 3171
www.renaissance.edu.vn

Saigon South International School
Tel: (+84-28) 3413 0901
www.ssis.edu.vn

Saigon Star International School
Tel: (+84-28) 3742 7827
www.saigonstarschool.edu.vn

Singapore International School
Tel: (+84-28) 3431 7477 and (+84-28) 3431 7472
www.kinderworld.net

The American School of Vietnam
Tel: (+84-28) 3519 2223
www.theamericanschool.edu.vn

Universities:

RMIT University
Tel: (08) 3776 1369
www.rmit.edu.vn

THINGS TO BUY BEFORE YOU ARRIVE

- High quality non-greasy sunscreen (imported and local sunscreen is available in Vietnam but I seem to get much more burnt when I buy sunscreen locally).
- An extra swimsuit, especially if you are larger than Asian-size. There are swimsuit tailors in Vietnam (which sounds very glam) but the finished product doesn't seem to have the *a-hem* support of store-bought suits, in my experience.
- Extra foundation. Even though it's hard to apply foundation when you're sweaty, it's nice for special occasions or if you're working. Big name cosmetics companies have a presence in Vietnam but they only sell products that suit Asian skin tones.
- Original documents – university degree, police checks, driver's license.
- Special medicines and vitamins (although some things are available here, it's best to be fully stocked when you arrive so you have time to source what you need).
- Large size clothes, shoes and underwear (you can get your favorite clothes copied by Vietnamese tailors once you're here and you can get shoes copied too but this can be a bit hit and miss).

WEIRD THINGS TO CONSIDER BRINGING WITH YOU

Sheets. For some reason, top sheets are hard to find in Vietnam. Even though I often have sets made by a sheet tailor (yes, they do exist!), but the fabric isn't the same as at home. High-end sheet sets are available in the upscale department stores, but they often don't have a top sheet either.

Cloth diapers/nappies. As far as I know, they're only sold secondhand in Vietnam by expats who no longer need them.

Swim diapers/nappies. Very difficult to source in Vietnam.

Toddler shoes. Sometimes it's easier to bring quality toddler shoes from home than spend days searching for a pair that aren't plastic, with squeakers in the soles and/or are covered in fake Disney characters.

Baby-proofing products. I have seen baby gates and have heard of people hiring carpenters to build baby gates at the top and bottom of stairs, but I have had no luck sourcing drawer and cupboard locks.

Easter eggs. Only available in the gourmet shops, and often sell out a few days before Easter (which is when you start thinking of Easter when you're not blasted with merchandising for months beforehand.)

Bike trailers. Baby seats are available at bicycle shops, but bicycle trailers have to be imported. So bring one with you if you plan to use one, but bear in mind trailers aren't really suited to Vietnamese traffic, except in the quietest expat areas.

Stain remover sticks. I have never been able to find these in Ho Chi Minh City and I stock up on Sard Wonder Sticks when I'm in Australia. The washing machines in Vietnam don't seem to work as well as the ones at home, and this is how I treat the grot accumulated by my greenthumb husband and our two dirty kids. Unfortunately, it doesn't work on sunscreen stains, but it does on most other things.

ACQUIRING WESTERN ITEMS IN VIETNAM
Vietnam's major cities, Hanoi and Ho Chi Minh City, have numerous expat-support services offering everything from French wine and cheese, Vegemite, organic granola, maple syrup, Australian beef,

Thai curry paste, Italian pasta, tins of baked beans, Danish shortbread, German sausages, and Czech beer to jars of American baby food. What can't be sourced in Vietnam can usually be ordered online, although some things do go missing in the post. Items imported by mail will attract import tax, with no apparent rhyme or reason to how the tax is calculated or any way of disputing the tax. As an example: the first time I ordered underwear from overseas I was not charged tax, the second time I was charged the equivalent of US$50, the third time US$1.50. In each case, the orders were for similar items (sports bras) totaling US$100 to US$150. In my case, over three attempts, the amount of tax averaged out to be quite acceptable.

EXPAT LIFE, SOCIAL CLUBS AND NETWORKING

The major cities all have their expat bars. The major tourist towns have their tourist/backpacker bars.

The expat experience in Vietnam is wildly varied. There are those who like to sit at cheap bars drinking beer every night, and there are those who never leave their expat enclave. Your experience in Vietnam is, to a large extent, up to you.

Some expats love Vietnam because the relatively low costs, which means they can live in a fancy house with a pool, a driver, a maid, a cook, a nanny and a security guard (which is, sadly, almost compulsory if you live in a fancy house). Others, like myself, love the cultural experience of living in a narrow alley in amongst the locals, driving a motorbike in the crazy traffic and eating snails and drinking beer on the footpath while sitting on child-size plastic furniture.

I can't speak highly enough of the free expat magazines, The Word HCMC, AsiaLife and Oi magazine. These resources list everything from sporting activities to bakeries and classes and ladies nights. It's how I know about swimsuit tailors, pony clubs, Japanese ice cream cafes, art galleries and the Hash House Harriers. Start asking around for the free magazines the minute your plane hits the tarmac in Vietnam.

Expat magazines

There are also numerous sporting clubs and formal and informal support groups.

Social clubs:

There is a plethora of social activities in Vietnam for expats, visitors and locals and any combination of the three.

> TIP: Sign up for meetup.com and see what local Meetups are happening close to you. There are new Meetup groups being formed every week, so you never know what opportunities might pop up. I have met some great friends at foodie, new mum/mom and working mum/mom meetups in three different countries.

Ho Chi Minh City

Hash House Harriers
Running/walking/drinking club that meets outside the Caravelle Hotel every Sunday at 2pm. Details at www.saigonh3.com.

International Ladies of Vietnam (Ho Chi Minh City)
An expat women's social group that organizes regular coffee dates (Thursdays, 10am at Purple Jade at the Intercontinental Hotel) as well as cultural, social and sporting activities. Regular activities include bridge, tennis, line dancing and mahjong.
http://ilvietnam.com

Idecaf
French cultural center and cinema
31 Thai Van Lung, District 1
Tel: (+84-28) 3829 5451
www.idecaf.gov.vn (French and Vietnamese)

Network Girls
Social group for professional women that meets monthly for breakfast or cocktails.
www.networkgirlshcmc.com

Hanoi

Institut Français de Hanoi - L'Espace
24 Trang Tien, Hoan Kiem
Tel: (+84-24) 3936 2164
www.ifhanoi-lespace.com (French and Vietnamese)

Goethe Institute
58 Nguyen Thai Hoc Street, Ba Đình
Tel: (+84-24) 373422525
www.goethe.de/hanoi

Hanoi International Women's Club
www.hanoi-iwc.com

> TIP: *Sports fans, do not fear, there are sport bars
> everywhere. I repeat, sport is everywhere.* There are bars in
> all the major expat and tourist centers throughout Vietnam
> where you can watch live broadcasts of sporty-things that
> have letters, such as NBL, AFL, MLB, UEFA, F1 and NRL.
> All I can say is ... thank goodness they also serve alcohol.

Websites/forums

TNH (previously The New Hanoian)
tnhvietnam.xemzi.com

Travelfish
www.travelfish.org

Vietnam Parents Network
http://groups.google.com/group/vietnam-parents-network

Anyarena
anyarena.com/en/

Online newspapers & magazines

AsiaLife HCMC
www.asialifehcmc.com

Oi Magazine (downloadable)
www.oivietnam.com

The Word Hanoi
www.wordhanoi.com

The Word HCMC
www.wordhcmc.com

Vietnam Economic News
news.vneconomy.vn/

Viet Nam News
vietnamnews.vnagency.com.vn

Thanh Nien News online
www.thanhniennews.com

Tuoi Tre News
tuoitrenews.vn

GROCERIES

Vietnam has two types of markets - wet markets and supermarkets.
Wet markets are usually large sheds or covered areas containing
many small stalls selling everything from meat, seafood, fruit,
vegetables, shoes, jewelry to flowers. Wet markets are usually
marginally cheaper than supermarkets but a lot more fun.

Wet markets are happy places

Vietnamese believe in the benefits of eating fresh food and it's not uncommon for the person responsible for cooking (the mother, grandmother or maid) to visit the market once, twice or even three times a day. Do as the locals do and get your fresh produce from your local market. Just remember to wash everything well, as Vietnamese farmers can be generous with pesticides. Washing with tap water is OK, just wipe the water off fruit and salad vegetables before you eat them.

Organic shops do exist. These are usually well-signed in English. There are also several shops in Hanoi and Ho Chi Minh City that stock all kinds of gourmet goodies and treats from home, no matter if you're homesick for Marmite, Vegemite or peanut butter and jelly.

Hanoi

Annam Gourmet (groceries and wine)
Syrena Tower, 51 Xuan Dieu St., Quang An Ward, Tay Ho Dist.
Tel : (+84-24) 6673 9661
www.annam-gourmet.com

Red Apron (wine shop)

28 Xuan Dieu, Tay Ho
Tel: (+84-24) 3719 8337

The Warehouse (wine shop)
Two locations: 59 Hang Trong, Hoan Kiem Ha Noi
Tel: (+84-24) 3928 7666
27 Xuan Dieu, Tay Ho District
Tel: (+84-24) 3718 3701
www.warehouse-asia.com

Bacchus Corner
1C Tong Dan, Hoan Kiem
Tel: (+84-24) 3935 1393

Hanoi Gourmet
6T Ham Long, Hoan Kiem
Tel: (+84-24) 3943 1009
www.hanoigourmet.com

Naturally Vietnam
4 Lane 67, Alley 12, To Ngoc Van, Tay Ho
Tel: (+84-24) 6674 4130
naturallyvietnam.com

The Oasis (Italian deli and butcher)
Three locations:
24 Xuan Dieu, Tay Ho
Tel: (+84-24) 3719 1196
18 Xuan Dieu, Tay Ho
Tel: (+84-24) 3718 6349
151 Thuy Khue, Tay Ho
Tel: (+84-24) 3728 6255
www.oasishanoi.net

Pane E Vino Wine Shop
3 Nguyen Khac Can, Hoan Kiem
Tel: (+84-24) 3826 9080

L's Place

Several locations, check the website for details
lsplace.com.vn

Veggy's
99 Xuan Dieu, Tay Ho
Tel: (+84-24) 3938 1769

Naturally Vietnam
No. 4, Alley 67, Lane 12, To Ngoc Van,
Tay Ho
naturallyvietnam.com

Ho Chi Minh City

Annam Gourmet
16-18 Hai Ba Trung St., Ben Nghe Ward, District 1
Tel: (+84-28) 3822 9332
www.annam-gourmet.com

Annam Gourmet An Phu
41A Thao Dien St., Thao Dien Ward, District 2
Tel: (+84-28) 3 7442 630 a

Annam Gourmet Phu My Hung
SB2-1 My Khanh 4, Ng Duc Canh, Tan Phong Ward, District 7
Tel: (+84-28) 5412 3263/64

Bacchus Corner (wine shop)
158D Pasteur, District 1
Tel: (+84-28) 3829 3306
bacchuscorner.com

100%
26B Thao Dien, District 2
Tel: (+84-28) 3519 4030
www.100percentvn.com

The Organik Shop
21 Thao Dien, District 2

Tel: (+84-28) 3744 6950
organikvn.com

Red Apron (wine shop)
22 Chu Manh Trinh, District 1
Tel: (08-8) 3823 0021
and
9A Thao Dien, District 2
Tel: (+84-28) 3 744 2363

Veggy's
29A Le Thanh Ton, District 1.
Tel: (+84-24) 3823 8526
Sky Garden, Pham Van Nghi, Bac Khu Pho, District 7
Riverside Apartments, 53 Vo Truong Toan, Thao Dien, District 2

Vino Wine Shop
74/17 Hai Ba Trung, District 1
Tel: (+84-28) 6299 1315

The Warehouse (wine shop)
15/5 Le Thanh Ton
District 1
Tel: (+84-28) 3825 8826
and
924 Tran Hung Dao,
District 5,
Tel: (+84-28) 6261 1526
www.warehouse-asia.com

An everyday Vietnamese supermarket (with frowny faces)

Costs

Life in Vietnam can be much cheaper than in developed countries, although it's possible to live quite lavishly, especially in Hanoi and Ho Chi Minh City. As you can see from the list below, fresh local items are substantially cheaper than imported items. After surveying friends and family at home and in Vietnam, I've included items that are regarded by some as comfort food, by others as essentials.

These prices were current as of November 2015 in Ho Chi Minh City. However, fruit and vegetable prices do fluctuate seasonally, and some imported items aren't always available.

Bread
Loaf of multigrain bread: VND87,000
Loaf of white bread: VND29,000
Six-pack of English muffins: VND101,000
French baguette: VND13,000
Local baguette: VND6,000
One croissant: VND20,000

Spreads
250g tub of butter (from France): VND124,000
250g tub of margarine (from Australia): VND120,000

340g jar of locally-made peanut butter: VND60,600
450g jar of Nutella: VND135,000
220g jar of Vegemite: VND167,000
375g jar of local guava jam: VND60,000
370 jar of French strawberry jam: VND111,000

Milk
Liter of fresh milk: VND44,000
1 liter tetra-pack of soy milk: VND29,600
Single serve tub of yoghurt: VND5,100

Cereal
275g pack of Kellogg's cornflakes: VND66,300
180g pack of Kellogg's Fruit Loops: VND70,000
500g Lowan (Australian brand) tropical museli: VND92,000

Meat
1kg pork: VND112,000
1kg chicken: VND110,000
1kg beef: VND260,000
1kg live prawns: VND343,000
1kg live lobster: VND1 million (a small lobster is usually 2kg)
Block of tofu: VND25,000
200g pack of smoked sliced ham: VND41,900
500g pack of hot dog sausages: VND80,900
500g pack of smoked bacon: VND116,000
185g can of tuna in oil: VND23,900
Whole roasted chicken (from Annam Gourmet): VND199,000

Cheese
Imported cheese (raclette from a gourmet shop): VND99,000/100g
Packet of 12 cheese slices: VND40,400
220g block of Bega Tasty cheese (from Australia): VND115,000
100g block of Payson Breton L'emmental (from France):
VND106,000
100g bag of locally-made parmesan-style cheese: VND70,000
8 portion pack of Laughing Cow cream cheese: VND45,000

Gourmet foods
Local pate: VND19,000/100g
180g jar of French duck pate: VND78,000
Mini quiche: VND50,000
Green olives (from the deli): VND115,000/100g
Marinated artichoke hearts: VND75,000/100g
100g of caviar: VND1.05 million
500g pack of imported Korean kimchi: VND70,000
23 fl oz jar of dill pickles: VND98,000
820g tin of peach halves in syrup (from Greece): VND100,000

Fruit and vegetables
170g pack of fresh strawberries: VND45,000
Fuji apples (from the US): VND81,000/kg
Mango: VND60,000/kg
Longan: VND60,000/kg
Durian: VND100,000/kg
Guava: VND15,000/kg
Watermelon: VND20,000/kg
Banana: VND33,000/kg
Bunch of fresh asparagus: VND38,000
2 cobs of fresh corn: VND14,000
2 leeks: VND9,000
1 celery: VND23,000
2 green peppers: VND17,000
2 red peppers: VND28,000
1 iceberg lettuce: VND18,000
Half head of broccoli: VND19,000
Carrots: VND16,000/kg
Onions: VND35,000/kg
Potato: VND49,000/kg
Small bunch of green onion/scallions: VND3,000
Large bag of mixed fresh herbs (basil, Vietnamese balm, perilla, fishwort) from a wet market: VND20,000
100g bag of parsley from a supermarket: VND10,000
100g bag of European basil from a supermarket: VND25,000
Bean sprouts for two people from the wet market: VND5,000

1kg pack of frozen mixed vegetables: VND60,300

Cooking staples
A dozen eggs: VND24,000
500g packet of flour: VND19,300
1kg pack of sugar: VND20,500
500ml bottle of imported olive oil: VND140,900
1 liter bottle of local vegetable oil: VND39,200
1kg rice: VND40,000
Packet of imported pasta: VND35,00
Packet of instant noodles: VND3,400
Bottle of ready-made pasta sauce: VND108,200
400g tin of tomato paste (from Italy): VND78,000
198g tin of tomato paste (from Vietnam): VND12,000
240g tin of diced tomatoes: VND27,000
425g tin of creamed corn: VND25,500
240g tin of red kidney beans: VND33,000

Convenience foods
37 oz box of pancake mix: VND100,000
500g pack frozen shrimp dumplings: VND39,000
500g pack frozen pork spring rolls: VND51,500
320g Frissta frozen pizza: VND90,000
400g tin of Heinz tomato soup: VND103,000

Condiments
500ml bottle of fish sauce: VND27,000
150ml bottle soy sauce: VND71,700
340g bottle of tomato ketchup: VND24,000
8 oz pack of American mustard: VND35,000
43g tube of wasabi paste: VND26,000

Baby items
Tin of Nestle infant formula: VND350,000
Small jar of baby food: VND42,000
Large jar of baby food: VND56,000

150g squeeze-pack of baby food: VND90,000
Pack of 54 Goo.n diapers, size L: VND473,000
Pack of 42 Huggies diapers, size L: VND205,000

Toiletries
320g bottle of Sunsilk shampoo: VND52,100
320g bottle of Sunsilk conditioner: VND52,100
140g tube of Colgate toothpaste: VND24,000
750g pack of Listerine mouthwash: VND126,000
Rexona roll-on deodorant for women: VND37,000
Rexona roll-on deodorant for men: VND41,000
Packet of 16 tampons: VND76,300
Packet of eight sanitary napkins: VND13,800
Packet of 12 condoms: VND122,000

Household items
2.7 kg pack of laundry liquid: VND169,000
1.8 litre pack of laundry softener: VND116,000
400g bottle of washing up liquid: VND10,400
750ml bottle of toilet cleaner: VND35,600
Plastic wrap: VND17,000
500g box of Whiskas dried cat food: VND132,000
Six-packet of toilet paper (3 ply): VND46,200
Can of Raid insect spray: VND65,000

Snacks and junk food
250g packet of plain crackers: VND20,300
Alpen brand raspberry and yoghurt museli bars: VND76,000
137g pack of Oreo cookies: VND10,700
110g tube of Pringles: VND30,200
100g Lindt milk chocolate bar: VND105,000
226g Hershey's Kisses: VND114,000
50g Tolberone bar: VND23,000
53g Mars Bar (made in Malaysia): VND21,000
31/4 oz packet of Doritos Cool Ranch corn chips: VND53,000
61/2 oz packet of Lay's BBQ chips: VND98,000
150g packet of Tyrrells Mature Cheddar Cheese and Chives crisps:
VND98,000

210g pack of jackfruit chips: VND57,000
500g tub of locally-made ice cream: VND120,000
160g packet of Haribo candy: VND47,000
1 macaron: VND30,000

Drinks
1.5 liter bottle of water from the supermarket: VND10,000
Can of Coca-Cola: VND8,200
1.5 litre bottle of Sprite: VND18,200
1 liter tetra-pack of apple juice: VND39,200
Packet of 25 Lipton tea bags: VND42,400
Packet of three-in-one instant coffee (20 sachets): VND42,900
200 gram pack of ground coffee (for Vietnamese fin coffee):
VND47,000
200g jar of Nescafe Red Cup instant coffee: VND108,000
250g pack of Lavazza ground Italian coffee: VND690,000
350g box of cocoa powder: VND160,000
400g jar of Milo: VND62,300

Alcohol
A can of Tiger beer from a supermarket: VND14,000
A bottle of Tiger beer from an upscale bar: VND70,000
Can of Budweiser from a supermarket: VND19,000
Bottle of Chimay from a supermarket: VND117,000
Bottle of Allan Scott Sauvignon Blanc 2014 from New Zealand from
the supermarket: VND397,000
Bottle of Allen Scott Sauvignon Blanc 2014 from New Zealand at
Xu bar: VND840,000
Bottle of Chateau Bouteilley 2012 Bordeaux from a wine shop:
VND395,000
Bottle of Tommasi Posecco from a wine shop: VND375,000
Bottle of Veuve Clicquot from a wine shop: VND1.52 million
70cl bottle of Jack Daniels No 7: VND676,000
750ml bottle of Johnny Walker Red Label: VND361,000

Dining out (Ho Chi Minh City prices)
Lotteria double-cheese burger: VND45,000
The James Brown Burger from Soul Burger: VND235,000.
Home delivered large Hawaiian pizza from Chez Guido:
VND169,000
Nine-piece nigiri sushi set at the Sushi Bar: VND110,000
One-person com plate at a *com tam* (broken rice) joint: VND30,000
Three-course set menu at La Villa French restaurant: VND990,000
Four-course food and wine discovery set at Propaganda Vietnamese
restaurant: VND520,000
Five-course set menu at Cyclo Resto Vietnamese restaurant:
VND125,000
Turkish breakfast set at Au Parc: VND195,000
Serve of *chạo tôm* (sugarcane shrimp) at Wrap & Roll:
VND85,000
Serve of bun cha at a local eatery: VND32,000
Serve of bun cha at Snap Cafe: VND130,000

Fuel
Liter of petrol/gasoline: VND21,300

Entertainment
Pirated new release movie DVD: VND15,000
Pirated boxed set of House, seasons 1-8: VND560,000
Pirated boxed set of Peppa Pig, seasons 1-4: VND100,000
Movie ticket for one adult (new release Hollywood film, subtitled in
English): VND90,000

Eggs and a happy egg vendor in a wet market in Ho Chi Minh City

Education and Child Care

One year at **Smart Kids**, Ho Chi Minh City
Early childhood (ages 18 months to 3.5 years) five full days a week:
US$10,150, plus a one-time non-refundable admission fee of
US$1,100
Big kids (ages 3 to 6 years) five full days a week: US$12,850, plus a
one-time non-refundable admission fee of US$1,100

One year tuition (up-front payment) at the **International School of
Ho Chi Minh City (ISHMC)**
Early explorers* (2 years, half days only): VND154,800,000
(US$7,200)
Kindergarten*: VND379,000,000 (US$17,625)
Year 7*: VND469,700,000 (US$21,840,000)
Year 12*: VND560,400,000 (US$26,000)
* Plus a one-time non-refundable admission fee of VND25,000,000
(US$1,165)

One year tuition (up-front payment) at **Ecoles Boulle et Billes**
(French language school)
Grade 1-3: VND95,000,000 (US$4,150), plus a one-time enrolment
fee of VND1.7 million (US$80)

One year tuition at the **British International School** (up-front payment)
Nursery: VND195,000,000 (US$9,065) plus a one-time non-refundable registration fee of VND21,700,000 (US$1,000)
Year 1*: VND374,000,000 (US$17,385)
Year 7*: VND461,000,000 (US$21,430)
Year 12*: VND528,900,000 (US$24,585)
* Plus a non-refundable registration fee of VND65,100,000

Medical

Standard GP consultation at Family Medical Practice: VND1.3 million (US$60)
Standard GP consultation at Victoria Healthcare: VND525,000 (US$25)

ELECTRICITY

The reliability of the electricity supply depends on where you are. There is a power shortage in Vietnam and many areas are subject to scheduled outages. The trick is finding out when the outages are scheduled. This is something you should check with your landlord. In one of the houses we lived in, the power was regularly cut on Sunday mornings from 9am to 1pm. In our new house, the power cuts seem more random and only seem to happen every few months.

We pay about $50 to $60 a month for electricity for our house in Ho Chi Minh City. We would pay substantially less if we didn't run the A/C in two bedrooms every night.

WATER
If you plan to stay long-term, you can organize delivery of 20/50 liter bottles of drinking water for household use. The most well-

known water delivery company is La Vie. You can organize delivery of big bottles of La Vie by calling (028) 930 0000 in Ho Chi Minh City and (024) 514 0000 in Hanoi.

HEALTH CARE

Vietnam has a number of Western standard clinics and hospitals catering for expats, tourists and upper-middle class Vietnamese citizens. The clinics offer everything from emergency medicine and outpatient services to obstetrics and psychiatric counseling.

There's also a range of alternative and complimentary health care services available, such as chiropractic care, acupuncture, and Chinese herbalists.

A Chinese herbalist at work in Ho Chi Minh City

A consultation with a Western doctor at one of the main Western clinics will set you back around $60. A consultation with a local doctor (who may well have trained overseas) can be as little as VND50,000. But finding an English-speaking doctors at local clinics can be difficult and too much of a daunting task when you feel sick. I take great comfort in the fact that world-class health facilities are available in Vietnam, even if they are a bit pricey.

There are also several international standard dental clinics in Vietnam with English-speaking staff. These dental clinics offer everything from basic cleaning to orthodontic work.

Hanoi:

Family Medical Practice
298 I Kim Ma, Ba Dinh
Tel: (+84-24) 3843 0748
www.vietnammedicalpractice.com

International SOS Hanoi
51 Xuan Dieu, Tay Ho
Tel: (+84-24) 3936 0666
www.internationalsos.com

L'Hospital Francais
1 Phuong Mai, Dong Da
Tel: (+84-24) 3577 1100 / Emergency: (+84-24) 3574 1111
www.hfh.com.vn

Vinmec International Hospital
458 Minh Khai, Hai Ba Trung
Tel: (+84-24) 3974 3556
www.vinmec.com

Westcoast International Dental Clinic
2nd floor, Syrena Center, 51 Xuan Dieu, Tay Ho
Tel: (+84-24) 3710 0555
westcoastinternational.com

Ho Chi Minh City:

CMI - Centre Medical International
1 Han Thuyen
District 1
Tel: (+84-28) 3827-2366

Columbia Gia Dinh International Hospital
1 No Trang Long
Binh Thanh District
Tel: (+84-28) 3803-0678

Columbia Saigon-24 Hours Clinic
8 Alexandre de Rhodes
District 1
Tel: (+84-28) 3823-8888

Family Medical Practice
Tel: (+84-28) 3822 7848
www.vietnammedicalpractice.com

FV Hospital
6 Nguyen Luong Bang, Saigon South (Phu My Hung), District 7
Tel: (+84-28) 3411 3333 (Emergency +84-28 5411 3500)
fvhospital.com

FV Saigon Clinic
3rd floor, Bitexco Financial Tower, 2 Hai Trieu, District 1
Tel: (+84-24) 6290 6167
fvhospital.com

Hanh Phuc Hospital
97 Nguyen Thi Minh Khai St, District 1
Tel: (84-28) 3925 9797
Binh Duong Boulevard, Binh Duong Province
Tel: (84-650) 363 6068
www.hanhphuchospital.com

Hospital of Traditional Medicine
187 Nam Ky Khoi Nghia
District 1
Tel: (+84-28) 3932-6579

Institute of Traditional Medicine
273-275 Nguyen Van Troi

Phu Nhuan District
Tel: (+84-28) 3997-1146

International SOS HCMC
(+84-28) 3829 8424
Vung Tau (+84-6) 4385 8776
Tel: (+84-28) 3823-8424
www.internationalsos.com

Victoria Healthcare International
79 Dien Bien Phu
District 1
Tel: (+84-28) 3910-4545
http://www.victoriavn.com/

American Chiropractic Clinic
8 Truong Dinh
District 3
Tel: (+84-28) 3930-6667
www.acc.vn

International SOS Dental Clinic
167A Nam Ky Khoi Nghai, District 3
Tel: (+84-28) 3829 8424
internationalsos.com

Starlight Dental Clinic
2 Bis Cong Truong Quoc Te, District 3
Tel: (+84-28) 3822 6222
starlightdental.net

West Coast International Dental Clinic
27 Nguyen Trung Truc, District 1
Tel: (+84-28) 3825 6999
and
Level 1, 71-79 Dong Khoi, District 1
Tel: (+84-28) 3825 6777
westcoastinternational.com

Hyperbaric chambers are located in Nha Trang, Quy Nhon and Vung Tau.

PET CARE

Many expats bring their furry family members to Vietnam when they relocate. Others acquire pets after they settle.

There's no quarantine requirement when importing a domestic cat or dog into Vietnam if the animal has:

- had a rabies vaccination between 30 days and 12 months prior to entry;
- a Vietnam International Health Certificate, completed by a vet accredited by the governing veterinary body of your home country, such as the United States Department of Agriculture (USDA) or the Canadian Food Inspection Agency (CFIA). This certificate states that the animal is healthy, free of parasites and that there is no evidence of diseases communicable to humans; and
- a rabies certificate. (Other vaccinations aren't required but if your pet is fully vaccinated, it would be a good idea to include the full records).

Altogether, these documents are considered a "pet passport" and they're all you should need to travel with your pet.

Once in Vietnam, the health of your pet will need some attention from a professional. From the anecdotes I've heard, the level of satisfaction with local pet care is mixed. As is the case in many areas of life, things are often done a little differently in Vietnam and some non-Vietnamese people find that quite vexing. There does seem to be many stories of vets overprescribing medicines for sick or injured pets. If you're worried about a vet pushing a lot of medicine on you, it's probably worth getting a second opinion.

I personally like the convenience of vets who make house calls for everything from post-surgery checkups to vaccinations.

It's worth noting that pet-napping is a widespread problem across Vietnam. Some thieves target dogs and cats to sell to dog and cat restaurants. Other petty criminals steal pets for the sole purpose of holding them for ransom. If you bring your pets to Vietnam, keep a close eye on them and make sure they don't roam the streets.

According to a *Thanh Nien News* report in March 2014, the Asia Canine Protection Alliance estimates 5 million dogs are killed every year in Vietnam for human consumption.

If your dog goes missing, put up posters in your local areas and let any local *xe om* drivers know of your pet's disappearance. Apparently offering a reward for the missing pet significantly increases the chances of the animal being returned. You can also visit (or ask a local to visit for you) one of the pet selling areas. In Ho Chi Minh City, it's Le Hong Phong Street in District 5 (between Hung Vuong and Tran Phu streets). In Hanoi, it's the Duong Kim Nguu Market.

Before you begin researching the logistics of bringing your fur-babies to Vietnam, look into the custom and quarantine regulations of your home country to make sure you can bring them back again. Australia, for example, does not allow the importation of domestic pets from Vietnam. You can send your pet home via a third country but the process is complicated and requires the animal to be given a rabies vaccine and subsequent test in the third country and then returning to Vietnam for a period of time before going back to the third country for six weeks or so.

The following vet clinics have English-speaking staff:

Ho Chi Minh City

Saigon Pet
33 Duong 41, Thao Dien, District 2

Tel: (+84-28) 3519 4182 or for emergencies (+84) (0) 909 063 267
www.saigonpet.com

New Pet Hospital
53 Dang Dung Street, District 1
Tel: (+84-28) 6269 3939
newpethospital.com.vn

Pet Care Hospital
124A Xuan Thuy Street, Thao Dien, District 2
Tel: (+84-28) 3523 4244

Veterinary Clinic Quang Vinh
187 Nguyen Thien Thuat Street, District 3
Tel: (+84-28) 3830 3489
www.bsvinh.com

There is a very active group in Ho Chi Minh City called Animal
Rescue and Care (www.arcpets.com) that encourages locals to adopt
unwanted or stray animals.

Hanoi

Happy Pet Clinic
103B, Lane 12, Dang Thai Mai, Tay Ho
Tel: (+84-24) 3718 3621
happypet.com.vn

ASVELIS Veterinary Hospital
D2-D4, 98 To Ngoc Van Street, Hanoi
Tel: (+84-24) 3718 2779
www.vietnampetservices.com

Pet Health
191 Au Co, Tay Ho District
Tel: (+84-24) 242 8882

Dr Bao (mobile vet)
Tel: (+84) (0) 903 223 217

WHAT TO WEAR

Here's a little bit more on this topic that's covered in the first part of this book, for those staying a little longer in Vietnam.

For women, shoulders and breasts should be covered for daytime outings. The Vietnamese are quite conservative, so coverage is important. Skin-tight jeans and t-shirts are acceptable on Vietnamese women until they reach a certain age (and I'm not sure what that age is). You'll find that Vietnamese women usually cover their shoulders for business and/or work situations. At night, feel free to show a bit more flesh but do take note of what the locals are wearing so you can work out what's appropriate (and age-appropriate) when you're socializing with Vietnamese people.

For men, long pants are required for business and formal outings. Shorts are considered the domain of old men. Shorts and singlets are definitely old man-style. If you want to be taken seriously, smart casual is the way to go. Suits if you want to impress but try to be smart about it – jacket on at the last minute and drink lots of water – no one will be impressed if you pass out from heat stroke.

Most schools advise foreign teachers to cover their shoulders and instruct them not to carry a backpack. Backpacking teachers have a bad reputation in Vietnam. They're considered unprofessional, unreliable and likely to disappear without giving notice. I found the no backpack rule a real pain when I was teaching English because a backpack is so handy when you're riding a motorbike.

My wardrobe is full of cotton, linen, and silk tops and pants, mostly made by local tailors. Visiting the tailor in Vietnam can be hit and miss, with some things never quite right. But the items are so much cheaper than what's available in the shops at home, so I just put up with the occasional tailoring mistake, like pants being too tight at the knees so they couldn't be worn on the motorbike. My biggest successes have been getting shirts copied, so at the moment I have the same style top in seven different fabrics.

Vietnamese people are very small and so the clothing in the shops is VERY small. Petite Western women have told me that although they could fit into Vietnamese clothes, most of the time the fit was never quite right, with arm holes tight and not enough bum-room.

Most Vietnamese people cover up when they're out in the sun. It's not uncommon to see women wearing evening-length gloves, a long-sleeved hoodie, socks (with high heeled sandals), a face mask and a sun bonnet over their motorbike helmet. Lately, women in Ho Chi Minh City have added to huge wrap-around skirts to this ensemble. Most of this gear is taken off upon arriving at the destination and stored under the motorbike seat.

BEING AWAY FROM FAMILY

Can be difficult because power and Internet can be unreliable. Facebook is regularly blocked by the government, although there are easy workarounds, which change as the government changes its tactics.

As mentioned in the tips section, Googling "Facebook blocked in Vietnam" will usually lead you to the latest workaround, which is often as simple as changing your computer's DNS code. And if you don't know how to do that, Google will have the answer as well.

Most expats have regular visits from friends and family and, depending on their budget, go home once a year. Many of the international schools have a long break in August, so Europeans and North Americans can head home for their summer.

Although some budget airlines such as Jetstar, Tiger and AirAsia service Vietnam, it's not always a cheap place to fly into or out of. If you're pricing flights, it's often worth checking the cost of flights out of the low-cost hubs of Bangkok, Kuala Lumpur and Singapore and then adding on the cost of budget flights to and from your destination in Vietnam.

CROSS-CULTURAL ADAPTATION

Vietnamese culture is very different from the Australian culture I grew up with. Vietnamese people are friendly and forgiving of most *faux pas* committed by foreigners.

I have worked for two Vietnamese companies, which gave me amazing insights into how things are done. The biggest cultural surprise for me was (and is) that Vietnamese people really do show respect to their elders. At after work drinks with the boss, the hierarchy is still very evident, with junior people being very deferential to senior people (especially when laughing at their not-so-funny jokes). I tried to talk to one boss as an equal, as is done in Australia, and he didn't quite know what to make of it. I'm part of a Vietnamese family now and I find the parent-child relationship quite formal, very different to the norm in Australia.

The biggest complaints that outsiders have when working in Vietnam is that Vietnamese people tend to have less developed forward planning and time management skills than people are used to. This can result in meetings called with only a few minutes notice and mad scrambles to get things done that, in hindsight, should have been well prepared for, such as nominating the official public holidays for *Tết*.

Living here with kids

Vietnamese people love kids. They express their love in ways that sometimes seem intrusive, especially if the child isn't enjoying the attention. Our kids have been pinched, poked, prodded and picked up uninvited. Their reactions have ranged from joyful laughter and free hugs to angry screams of protests ... and people's response are always the same -- indulgent smiles.

When either of the kids are not happy with the attention, I usually have to rescue them because their Vietnamese fans think temper tantrums are as adorable as giggles. When I deal with Vietnamese kids, I always back off if they look worried or upset (or scared of my devil-blue eyes) and I feel frustrated that Vietnamese adults don't act the same way towards my precious little ones. But after saying that, I have to stress that the good vastly outweighs the bad when it comes to kids.

When we went out to dinner with our babies, waitresses used to pick them up and carry them around the restaurant. Now that our daugher is is a bit older (and more easily bored during grown-up dinners at restaurants), we take toys and coloring books. Sometimes she will play happily alone or with a new-found little friend, and sometimes the wait staff will play with her. We've had three waiters sit down around her and "help" (as in do it for her) her complete an entire coloring book as if it was homework. We've also had waiters and waitresses play rowdy games of chase with the kids -- the noise is all just part of daily life here.

One thing I really love here is that the pedophile paranoia is yet to make an appearance. While I'm sure this kind of sexual deviance exists, there is no widespread assumption that every man who smiles at or touches a child in public has evil ulterior motives. So in Vietnam it's OK for my husband to wrestle and tickle the kids at the child care center, even though he hasn't met them before and doesn't know their parents. It's also OK for the motorbike parking guy at our favorite cafe to kiss and cuddle my daughter when he helps her off my bike. (I would, of course, be a bit worried if I heard about a stranger kissing or cuddling my daughter when no one was around.)

(Note the strange penis-grabbing tendencies of some Vietnamese people in the countryside, as mentioned in the tips section of this book.)

There are plenty of activities for older kids - everything from horseback-riding and music classes to tae kwon do and stage schools. There are also swimming pools and cinemas and shopping malls with arcade games for teens who need to just hang out with friends.

Pros/cons

Life in Vietnam can be amazing, full of fun and interesting new people. But it can also be hard work at times.

I know some trailing spouses struggle with their sense of worth when they arrive, feeling very isolated once the kids are at school, the breadwinner is at work and there's no one around to share the challenges of negotiating shopping, cooking, cleaning, building a social life and handling domestic staff as well as other Vietnamese oddities, such as the people who sift through your rubbish looking for recyclables.

A Vietnamese recycling lady doing her rounds

My only advice is to tackle your new life in Vietnam the same way you would a new job. You have to work at it, building a network and a knowledge base so that you have a life you're comfortable with. Some expats live a mostly "foreign" life in fancy air-conditioned houses, flitting between Western style cafes and restaurants in chauffeur-driven cars. Others have a very local life, living in a back alley, shopping at wet markets, driving motorbikes and dining on tiny tables and chairs at sidewalk eateries. The beauty about living in Vietnam is that it's possible to enjoy an amazing mix of local life and the high life.

A wet market butcher at work

My years in Vietnam have been some of the best of my life. However, I have had a few black days, times when I needed a friendly ear to have a rant about the difficulties of living here. Sometimes my Vietnamese husband would understand my frustration, other times he just couldn't comprehend what the problem was.

Pros:
It's cheap. The cost of food, beer and accommodation is a fraction of what it is in Western countries. On a salary that wouldn't pay the rent at home, it's possible to live quite well, going to fancy restaurants, up-market bars, taking trips out of town and living in a nice apartment or house.

It's fun. Vietnamese people seem much more playful than Westerners. An almost childlike sense of humor prevails and it's not uncommon to see grown men slapping their legs and doubling over in laughter watching a rerun of an old Tom & Jerry cartoon (that they've probably seen before) on a battered television in the corner of a noodle restaurant.

There's an energy. No matter what hour of the day or night it is, there are people working -- working to better their lives or feed their families or get ahead, from government employees sweeping the streets after midnight to entrepreneurial types prowling the streets in the wee hours with home-made metal detectors to collect screws and other junk to sell to scrap dealers.

Cons:
It's cheap. Sometimes it can seem like nothing is ever done to the standard you're used to. Even building a flight of steps so each riser is the same height seems to be something Vietnamese builders and engineers don't really strive for. Things often break, break down, explode or inexplicably stop working.

It's noisy. The noise of traffic and construction are almost inescapable. Even if you move into the quietest of the quietest hems, Murphy's Law says that a week after you move in the neighbors will decide to tear their house down and build a new one.

TOP TIPS

Be patient, be tolerant and try to understand what's happening around you.

Keep your expectations low to avoid disappointment. Vietnam is

NOT the same as home and things work differently here. The local way isn't wrong or stupid, it's just the local way.

Make at least one local friend who can answer your questions. Tell this friend you need someone to explain the country, and use this person as a sounding board. Rather than getting irritated or angry by local practices and customs, ask this person to explain why something is the way it is. Often, when you understand the background or the tradition, things are not so annoying.

For example, I was incredibly frustrated by getting vague or unhelpful answers from work colleagues until someone told me that in Vietnam it's rude to say no. So people evade the question or lie in order not to appear rude. Once I knew that, I could preface my requests by – "tell me if it's not possible, please don't try to be polite, I need to know." It was still hard for my colleagues to tell me no, but things were so much easier when we were aware of the gulf and could make an effort to meet halfway.

Cover up tattoos. In the past, it was only gangsters, prostitutes and "fast" girls who had tattoos. That is changing, but I think it's better to avoid falling into these stereotypes when people are making their first impression of you.

FINAL THOUGHTS ON LIVING IN VIETNAM

Vietnam is chaotic and noisy, filled with people who seem oblivious to the chaos and noise. It can seem overwhelming at first but once your senses adjust, you will find pockets of tranquility and a myriad of things to fascinate you.

It's a country on the move, governed by a Communist government obsessed with economic development and progress. There are construction sites everywhere, from suburban backstreets to city centers and along the national highway. All this progress just contributes to the noise, of course.

As a result of the government's push to move Vietnam towards a market economy, entrepreneurialism is everywhere. This individual quest for profit results in shops and restaurants popping up, moving and closing down with incredible speed. It also results in a very high turnover of staff, as everyone is always ready to take a chance on a new opportunity, either as an employee or an entrepreneur themselves.

Every day in ways you couldn't possibly imagine, there are examples of Vietnamese resourcefulness. From the way motorbikes are used to transport towering loads to the methods used in construction, Vietnamese people are using cheap, cheerful and ingenious workarounds. And most of the time they work, too. One of my favorite examples of Vietnamese resourcefulness is the slip-on backless men's business shoe that looks like a proper shoe from the front and a pair of slippers from the back.

In the midst of all this industry and go-getting, there's a lightheartedness to Vietnamese people that seems to have been forgotten by most of the Western world. It can be very endearing. When I see this playfulness in action, it's a reminder that I should not be taking life too seriously because it means missing out on some of life's fun.

Vietnamese people have a certain innocence that's been replaced by weary cynicism in many other countries. Although sometimes unaware of how things work outside of Vietnam -- the result of the country being closed for 20 years -- most people are interested in foreigners as individuals and as representatives of their home countries.

All in all, Vietnam is an amazing country. It's survived centuries of war, deprivation and foreign rule and yet there is no sense of being downtrodden or victorious. It can seem crazy and nonsensical at times but if you take the time to find out why some things are the way they are, there's almost always a reason (which can be a crazy reason, but it's still a reason).

I came to Vietnam as a burnt-out career girl, uncertain of what the future might hold. Vietnam restored my sense of perspective, reminding me of what's important in life - family, health, friends and good food. This country also gave me a husband and children and amazing opportunities that I would never have considered at home. Vietnam will always have a place in my heart and in my life ... and I think that's a sentiment shared by many non-Vietnamese people who live and work in Vietnam for a time.

Sunrise on Con Dau Island

Acknowledgments:

I could not have written this book without my co-author, photographer and everyday sidekick, Vu. He has been my personal tour guide for more than seven years. With him, I have explored Vietnam and other parts of Southeast Asia, as well as other non-location specific destinations such as parenthood, cross-cultural coupledom and expat life. Vu has been my translator and photographer as I've explored -- and fallen in love with -- Vietnam, with blogging and with writing again after being burnt out by journalism. Thank you, darling man, for putting up with me while I chased such elusive goals.

Many thanks also to Winnie Lam, Julie Stockwell, Sarah Martin, Kate Brayley, Robyn Adam, John Burns, Willow Tesseneer, David Bell, Diane Anthony, Van Pham, Rosariet Swagemakers and Sonja Everson who advised, proof read and assisted in various other ways with this book, which took several years to take from a concept to a reality.

Resources & references

CIA Vietnam Factbook
https://www.cia.gov/library/publications/the-world-factbook/geos/vm.html

www.vietnamembassy-usa.org

http://www.austrade.gov.au/Doing-business-in-Vietnam/default.aspx
-- The doing business guide is a must-read for anyone traveling to Vietnam, even if you're not planning to do business. A quick and practical guide to some cultural differences that crop up in business, it's a handy insight for those planning an extended stay.

http://www.austrade.gov.au/Vietnam-profile/default.aspx

Human Rights Watch World Report 2015 – Vietnam chapter
https://www.hrw.org/world-report/2015/country-chapters/vietnam

United Nations country overview:
http://www.un.org.vn/en/about-viet-nam/overview.html

World Bank country profile:
http://web.worldbank.org/WBSITE/EXTERNAL/COUNTRIES/EASTASIAPACIFICEXT/VIETNAMEXTN/0,,menuPK:387573~pagePK:141132~piPK:141121~theSitePK:387565,00.html

http://data.worldbank.org/indicator/SE.ADT.LITR.ZS

http://sgtvt.hochiminhcity.gov.vn/web/tintuc/default.aspx?cat_id=592&news_id=4501

Centre for Disease Control:
wwwnc.cdc.gov/travel/destinations/vietnam.htm

http://www.indochinacapital.com/investing_in_vietnam.php

Hanoi International Women's Club: http://hanoi-iwc.com

Hello Saigon: http://hello-saigon.com

The Word Vietnam: http://www.wordhcmc.com/

AsiaLife Ho Chi Minh City: http://www.asialifemagazine.com/

Authors

Barbara Adam is an Australian political and financial journalist who took a "three months or so" working holiday in Vietnam in 2007. The working holiday has continued to this day, taking her from Vietnam to Singapore and Thailand and back to Vietnam. Highlights of her holiday (which has gone on long enough now for her to call it a lifestyle) include working at Vietnam's two leading media organizations, meeting the most handsome man in Vietnam and starting a family with him. Barbara has experienced Vietnam as a single party girl, part of a courting couple and as the parent of small children and she has loved every stage of her Vietnam life. Barbara and her Vietnamese husband Vu run street food tours in Ho Chi Minh City (www.saigonstreeteats.com) and she blogs about her new life at www.thedropoutdiaries.com.

Vu Vo is a marketing manager whose life has never been the same since he met a loud and rambunctious Australian girl in early 2008. That meeting caused some serious problems for his expected career trajectory, turning him into a country-hopping stay-at-home-dad, tour guide, author, photographer and business owner. None of these unexpected roles, however, affected his ability to be relaxed yet quietly bossy. Vu comes from a foodie family - his parents run a small *cháo* and *bún bò Huế* restaurant near Vung Tau - and, like his his four brothers and one sister, Vu is an enthusiastic and opinionated home cook.

Cover photo:

Our cover model, Miss Dang, is one of the drivers for our street food tours. She has just completed a Bachelor of Finance from the Ho Chi Minh City University of Economics and we know she has a fabulous career ahead of her in the world of business. She was sweet enough to pose for us at a local temple, wearing a friend's old school uniform and a cage of birds that someone just happened to leave in the doorway when we were doing our photoshoot.

(Photo by Vu Vo)

Made in the USA
San Bernardino, CA
08 April 2016